WHERE THE

CW00917422

WHERE THERE'S
A WILL

by
MAURICE BARBANELL

THE AQUARIAN PRESS

This edition first published 1988
First published in 1952 by Spiritualist Press

British Library Cataloguing in Publication Data

Barbanell, Maurice
Where there is a will.
1. Personal success — Manuals
I. Title
158'.1

ISBN 0-85030-753-8

*The Aquarian Press is part of the
Thorsons Publishing Group, Wellingborough,
Northamptonshire, NN8 2RQ, England*

Printed in Great Britain by Richard Clay Limited,
Bungay, Suffolk

2 4 6 8 10 9 7 5 3 1

CONTENTS

FOREWORD

IT was Tennyson who put into the mouth of Ulysses the words, "I am a part of all that I have met." This description may well serve for the pages that follow.

Whistler once explained that the comparatively high fees he demanded for his paintings were not based on the time taken to execute them but on the years of experience and knowledge that preceded every finished canvas.

This book is the result of a search for truth that has so far lasted thirty years and, naturally, still continues. I have combed the religions and philosophies of East and West and taken into account, so far as I comprehend them, the views of modern science.

If I were able to give the source of all the information this book contains, it would fill another volume. But even that is an impossible task. For as long as I can remember, I have been a voracious reader, fascinated by the printed word. I belong to the category of those who cannot resist reading all the printed matter that comes into their possession.

Where I have made a direct quotation, I have given the source, so far as I have records. If there be any authorities or authors to whom I have not done justice, I ask for their forgiveness in advance, if they are still on earth. If not, the matter can be adjusted elsewhere. The rest of my information comes from the many hundreds of books, and from many thousands of newspapers, journals and magazines, often with the names of the writers not disclosed. I have been blessed with a retentive memory and I have dipped freely into my mental storehouse for the compiling of this book.

I trust that I will not be considered vain if I declare that at times, alas too few, I have been conscious of "help from the unseen," the source of all inspiration, for which I express my gratitude. I pray that I have not been too unresponsive a channel and that some of the wisdom of the unseen, which I have sought to capture, helps those who are seeking the way to a fuller life.

I cannot claim any originality for the ideas I express in this book, for, of course, "there is nothing new under the sun." What I have attempted is to portray what I regard as vital truths, known, unfortunately, only to a minority in all the ages and in our own day.

I know that, when the precepts described in these pages are put into practice, life becomes a great and stimulating adventure.

CHAPTER I

THE CHALLENGE

WHY do some succeed and others fail? Why do some face life with confidence, ready to meet every challenge, while others dread the coming of a new day? Why do some enjoy radiant health, while others do not know what it is to feel well?

These are not insoluble mysteries. There are intelligent answers to these vital questions. You can enjoy life, once you understand the plan of existence. Yes, there is a plan. You can learn how to abolish fear, worry and anxiety, and how to satisfy *all* your needs. There is an infinite storehouse to which you can have access, and it has a limitless supply.

These are realities, based on the operation of natural laws that cannot fail. Millions live in the darkness of ignorance when the sunlight of knowledge is theirs for the asking. Literal truths are expressed in the words: "Ask, and it shall be given you; seek, and ye shall find; knock, and it shall be opened unto you." And you can begin to put these injunctions into practice now.

9

There are no insuperable handicaps, no barriers that cannot be overcome. Whoever you are, and wherever you may be, you can call to your aid the greatest powers in the universe. You can obtain strength to conquer every weakness and guidance for every problem. Health, happiness and prosperity can be yours. If your life is a raging turbulence, you can find peace. If everything seems futile, you can discover purpose. If your existence is drab and monotonous, you can have colour and variety.

You were intended to have a rich, full life. Within you are the means to achieve it. You possess all the necessary equipment. God has given you the tools so that you can finish the job. That, indeed, is why you are here on earth.

First, you must learn who and what you are. You must realise that you are not your body, that you are mind and spirit, that you are the repository of infinite possibilities. There are laws and forces, far superior to anything that is material, which you can utilise, once you learn to live in harmony with them.

You can be the master and not the slave of circumstance. Abolish the thought that you are insignificant, a nonentity, and realise that you are the apex of creation, the crown of evolution. You are part of the infinite, divine power which fashioned the immeasurable universe and all that it contains, be it majestically mighty or microscopically minute.

When you learn to live in harmony with this power, you will derive from life the richness, lustre and nobility which are your rightful heritage—and you will fulfil your divine destiny.

CHAPTER II

TURNING ON THE SWITCH

YOU can achieve all that you desire—if you really desire it. But you must have complete and unwavering confidence that achievement will be yours. It is the possession of what amounts almost to perfect faith that defeats many people.

To the individual with a single, inflexible purpose, obstacles are not deterrents. They are challenges which he knows he can meet. These do not lessen his determination; they increase it, if that be possible. His mind is always set on the goal of his achievement. He refuses to be deflected.

This unwavering determination sets into motion certain forces which, whether he knows it or not, help him to realise his objective. That is the secret of success. Within man there is an infinite power which the majority seldom call into action, and then only in times of stress or crisis.

In the invisible atmosphere, there is also a tremendous dynamic power waiting to be utilised by those who know how to co-operate with it. The existence of these forces, within and without, have been known to some through the ages. It explains the "miracles" wrought in ancient days and the revelations received by seers and saints. It explains the inspiration which comes to artists, poets, musicians, dramatists, writers and orators. It explains the wonders performed by hypnotists, yogis and fakirs. It explains the "hunches" of the successful business man. It explains the premonitions which have saved people from disaster.

There never have been miracles in the sense that natural laws were superseded, suspended or abrogated. The universe is controlled by unchanging natural laws, which is another way of saying that God is the same yesterday, today and forever. Any wonders performed by men centuries ago can be repeated by men today.

The secret of life is to live in harmony with nature's laws and to reap the rich results, spiritually, mentally and materially. You must try to understand, so far as you can, how these laws operate. You must appreciate who and what you are, the purpose of earthly life and the nature of the world in which you live.

Knowledge will enable you to chart and steer your course. There is, of course, a limit to the knowledge that you can acquire. Knowledge, like the universe, is infinite, and the human capacity to receive and to assimilate it is subject to certain limitations. A pint jug cannot hold a gallon of milk. But you can remove many limitations and increase your mental capacity.

Faith will help you sometimes where knowledge cannot reach. You do not have to know what electricity is in order to turn on the switch, or plug your apparatus into the main power. You have made a tremendous step forward when you *know* that by turning on the switch *the power will come*. Both within and without, the great power is always there. It will always come when you learn how to turn on the switch.

When obscured by dense fog, the pilot of an aircraft realises that if he tunes in to ground control, radar will guide him to the runway path. He need not know how radar works, only that it does. His contribution is to receive directions from unseen operators, in whom he has complete confidence, and to follow them till he is safely home.

You have access to a power immeasurably greater than electricity or radar. If you tune in correctly, and turn on the switch, it will guide and help you; it will bring you health, happiness, prosperity, in fact, all that you desire. But you must understand the nature of your own being. You must be brought face to face with yourself. You must begin by seeking the answer to the fundamental question, "Who am I?"

To give your name, or to produce a birth certificate, is not the answer. Nor is the reply a description of your face, the colour of your hair and eyes, your height and weight and other distinctive physical characteristics. These describe your body; *but you are not your body.* You are not a collection of cells, nerves, muscles, tissues and sinews. You are not your legs, arms, stomach, lungs, heart or liver.

It is generally accepted that the cells of the body are completely changed every seven years. But *you* do not change every seven years. Your body is no more you than the violin is the violinist, the typewriter the typist, or the pen the writer. Your body is the mechanism by which you express yourself. Your body is the means by which physical sensations are conveyed to you through the five organs of sense.

Your eyes register vibrations of light, just like the lens of a camera when the shutter is opened. The camera does not see. You see, because you have a mind with powers of perception. The process of seeing is not accomplished until you have perceived the object.

Your body does not think, reflect, judge, decide, plan, wonder, revere, appreciate, love, hate, envy or sorrow. These are all mental operations. Your brain is not your mind. Your brain is physical; your mind is non-physical. A physical brain cannot produce non-physical substance.

You think. Thought cannot be weighed, touched, seen, heard, smelt or tasted. Yet thought is real. So are all the attributes of your mind. But even your mind does not think. *You* think with your mind.

Who are you? You are "something" with a mind and a body. You are an individuality, a consciousness, a spirit. That is it—you are a spirit.

What do I mean by a spirit? We have to use words which are, after all, material symbols to explain what is non-material and is far superior. Words can never convey the entirety of the ideas they are trying to express.

To those who have investigated, there is unassailable evidence that man survives death. Well-attested communications reveal that man continues to manifest, in the after-life, as a distinct individual, that he possesses memory, consciousness, affection and love, and that he makes himself known through a body which is

just as real and "solid" as its physical counterpart.

Where conditions are appropriate, and this is
the essential pre-requisite, those who survive are
able to give guidance, which will be received
consciously or unconsciously, by the ones they
love. Indeed, we are always surrounded by love
which is prepared to break down all the barriers
to make itself known.

The so-called dead do not persist as material
beings, for the physical body has perished. They
say, and they ought to know, that they survive
as spiritual entities and that Survival is part of
of the natural law. I recall the Irishman who
aptly summarised the situation by saying, "You
can't die for the life of you!" Survival is not a
reward for a good life, or a punishment for a bad
one—it has no connection with our religious
views, or lack of them.

The natural law operates and we are born. It
operates again and the body dies, but we continue as spiritual beings. It is not death which
confers a spiritual nature upon us. Death is
powerless to touch the spiritual nature which we
have always possessed.

The inference is simple; we are spiritual beings
here and now. We live because we are spirit.
Spirit is the mainspring of our existence. The

body is animated by our spirit. Life is spirit, and spirit is life. Moreover, we are not bodies with spirits, but spirits with bodies, a distinction with a great difference.

"God is spirit," says the Bible, which means that in essence we are related to the power behind all universal activity. We are cast in the divine mould, made in the divine likeness. "And God breathed into man and he became a living soul." As spirit, you have access to the infinite powers of an infinite God. Albeit in miniature, you possess all the divine attributes.

The relationship between spirit, mind and body now becomes clearer. You are a being living simultaneously on three planes of expression. The mind's relationship to the spirit is similar to the brain's relationship to the body.

The purpose of life is to develop all three aspects of your nature. Evolution accomplishes part of its divine and natural purpose when the body, having ripened through experience, falls away, just as the apple drops from the tree when it is ripe. Then the individual is ready for the next inevitable stage, the life beyond what is called death.

Once you visualise yourself as a spirit with a body, the trials and problems of daily existence are seen in a different perspective. And once you realise the latent mental and spiritual powers that you possess, you can transform the whole of your future and master your own fate.

There is no rigid line of demarcation between spirit, mind and body, or between spiritual, mental and physical activities. The universe is one; all life is one, each aspect blending and harmonising with the other.

You are surrounded by a pulsating, teeming life that you cannot see or hear, simply because your physical senses are limited in their range of reception. The telescope, microscope, radio, radar, infra-red and X-ray apparatus enable you to register some of these vibrations which are either too slow or fast for your eyes and ears.

Deliberate development of your innate faculties will enable you to capture some of the beauties and wonders of the larger life round and about you. Many gifted and sensitive people have already done so. The possession of extra-sensory perception has been proved by thousands of experiments. And are we not all familiar with the fact that blind people have developed an added faculty of "sensing" which the majority of sighted mortals must possess but never use?

A friend of mind, a policeman, on patrol duty on a night when dense fog made him almost lose his way, was asked by a pedestrian to direct him to a certain street. The fog made it impossible to give any indications that would be of any help. Just then, a blind man arrived, tapping with his stick. The fog was no obstacle to him. A memory, sharpened by loss of sight, with his added gift of sensing, enabled him to take the pedestrian by the arm and guide him to his destination.

What you have to do is take charge of your mind, "turn on the switch" and harness your latent powers, which are waiting to be developed. Many systems of memory training operate by utilising the powers of the subconscious mind. Mental discipline will eradicate bad habits and create good ones. Thousands of people dispense with alarm clocks. They tell their subconscious mind the time they want to awaken and it follows the instruction to the minute. You might well ask how it knows the time, but the answer is that it does.

Your mind plays an important part in your health. Those who are always afraid of getting some illness become "disease conscious" and help to attract what they fear. Just as those who think always in terms of health are helping to attract health. It is simply a question of attunement to the natural forces, to "turning on the switch."

Mind and body are subject to constant inter-action. While it is true that the body restricts and affects the mind, it is equally true that the mind directs, develops and controls the body. Matter is the servant, not the master of the mind.

Many actions that you perform mechanically were originally due to the definite will and desire exercised by the mind. When you began to learn to walk, your mind had to call on all the necessary nerves and muscles to co-ordinate their activities. Your first steps were due to a delib-erate, conscious mental projection of the deter-mination to walk. Now, when you wish to walk, the conscious mind flashes the request to your subconsciousness and the required machinery is automatically set into motion.

A similar process occurs with almost all your bodily activities. The task of directing them has been relegated to your subconscious mind, which is the repository of all that were originally con-scious thoughts and desires.

Your subconscious mind will work for you in many other directions, once you have given it the necessary instructions. It is simply waiting for your commands, which it will obey without question. It does not work on its own accord. You must provide the initial stimulus.

The mind is king, and thought is its most potent weapon. Yet how lacking in mental power are the vast majority of human beings! They do not know how to concentrate or control their own minds, to regulate their thoughts, or even how to relax properly.

Consider the feats performed by yogis and fakirs. After years of strict discipline, they have achieved complete mental mastery of their bodies. They can make themselves immune to pain, even though unsterilised hat pins are pierced through their throats and palms, and they can prevent the flow of blood when these operations are performed. They can lie on beds of sharp nails and feel no ill effects.

They can induce cataleptic trances and make their bodies so rigid that an individual can walk on them when their forms are suspended between two chairs. And they experience no pain. They can regulate the beating of their hearts and pulses, making them slower or faster than normal. They can walk on red-hot embers without being burnt. They can be buried alive and emerge without a trace of suffering. I saw many of these feats demonstrated by one fakir in a London hall when the results were attested by medical men.

What a tribute is all this to the potency of

thought! And the fact that others can master their bodies means that you too can do so.

Almost everything in life begins with the mind. Long before the architect's plans are drawn they exist in his mind's eye. All creative work is an attempt to materialise what the mind has already "seen." Deaf Beethoven transferred to paper compositions that he had already "heard" in his mind. The gifted author often has his plot complete before he writes one word. Great writers have described how their characters took mental shape and the novelists became merely the instruments for recording their adventures.

Our minds do not sleep when our bodies slumber. They continue to manifest, albeit in a time-space relationship that is vastly different from our physical environment. We span oceans and continents, live through "years" of experiences, all in a matter of minutes, or is it seconds?

In many hypnotic experiments, the mind, released from the body, has travelled vast distances, and has returned to describe what it has seen. Inquiry has subsequently confirmed the out-of-the-body experiences. Some people have the ability to leave their bodies at will. The famous writer, William Gerhardi, who possesses this faculty, has devoted a fascinating book to his superphysical travels. Camille Flammarion, the distinguished French astronomer, has recorded, in three published volumes, many hundreds of authenticated examples of mental messages received and visions seen, sometimes when thousands of miles separated the people concerned.

Telepathy demonstrates that mind can communicate with mind without utilising the five physical senses. The most feasible explanation seems to be that operator and subject are on similar mental wavelengths and can tune in to one another.

Yet thought is a mystery. What is it? Where does it emanate? What is its composition? I contend that we do not create or originate thought. Indeed, we do not create anything in the sense that we make something out of nothing. We take something that exists and change its form. We know nothing about first causes, either in the spiritual, mental or physical realm.

There is some quality in us that determines the thoughts that we receive. We are like human radio sets, except that we can both transmit and receive thoughts. Just like the radio set, we have a certain range of reception, but the comparison is not altogether adequate *because we can increase our range of reception*. By training and development we can attract far more than we normally entertain.

There is no need to be a crystal-set mind. By "turning on the switch," you can receive a power that will transform the whole of your life. Mind is the most colossal power in the world.

CHAPTER III

MIND AND BODY

HOW little is still known of the mind's potentialities or its relationship with the body. The connection between physical health and mental states has been realised for years and is now receiving increasing attention. Medical research workers have compiled, under the heading of psychosomatics, a long list of diseases which owe their origin solely to mental causes. One outstanding example is that duodenal ulcers begin with worry.

It has long been emphasised that indigestion and other stomach upsets arise more often through worry and overstrain than any other factors. I have seen quoted the statement that doctors incline to the view that sixty per cent. of all our ills are outside the provisions of medicine.

In his book, *The Anatomy of Happiness*, Dr. Martin Gumpert declares that two-thirds of the patients who visit consulting rooms are not organically sick. They complain about nervousness, fatigue, insomnia and headaches, but often, he writes, "it is *fear* that is affecting their bodies, gradually changing an abnormal emotional state into an organic physical disease."

Another doctor relates the case of a patient admitted to hospital suffering from incipient glaucoma, a clouding over of the eye that can quickly lead to blindness. A chance comment in the consulting room led the patient to break down and cry for the first time for many years. Not long afterwards, all traces of glaucoma completely disappeared. The man had not really been going blind, but by some psychological twist he had prevented himself from crying. "Such successes are common once the patient can be persuaded to burst into tears," says the doctor who treated him, "for unrestrained weeping is often the first step towards health and happiness."

Psychological problems often produce physical defects, as is borne out in the case of left-handed children who, when compelled to use their right hand, immediately begin to stammer. Similarly, many types of industrial illnesses, in which the patients suffer from cramps, twitches, tremors and even worse troubles, have developed quite unconsciously because they were bored with their jobs and wanted to be transferred to something else.

Professor John Ryle, of Radcliffe Infirmary, Oxford, has put on record his view that more than forty per cent. of the people suffering from coronary thrombosis, which accounts in Britain for 36,000 deaths in an average year, brought this disease on themselves by severe emotional strain.

A sense of guilt will also produce physical illness. Once this has been removed by the psychologist, health usually follows. This truth was known in Bible days, when Jesus accomplished a cure by telling the sick man to sin no more.

If worry and fear and anticipating the worst could be eradicated, more people would enjoy good health. Anticipation is generally worse than the event itself. Besides, it is the unexpected that nearly always happens. And nothing is ever gained by fear and worry.

When Dr. William H. Bates, an American eye specialist, invented a system based on relaxation and certain exercises to improve sight, orthodox oculists opposed his technique. They argued that it was far-fetched to assert that relaxing the mind could affect the physical structure of the eyes. "But now," according to medical testimony, "there is hard evidence that almost every tissue in the body can be damaged by mental stress. Most doctors are convinced that ailments of the heart and lungs are undoubtedly aggravated by worry. So are skin complaints."

In *Man, The Unknown*, Dr. Alexis Carrell, the scientist and surgeon who was awarded the Nobel Prize for his work in suturing blood vessels and the transplantation of organs, writes that envy, hate and fear, when these are habitual sentiments, are capable of starting organic changes and real diseases. Health, he says, can be profoundly disturbed by moral suffering. Business men who do not know how to fight worry die young. In specially sensitive people, striking modifications of their bodily tissues are induced by their emotions.

He quotes the case of a woman on whose arm an eruption appeared during a bombardment. The eruption became redder and larger after each shell exploded. These phenomena, he asserted, were far from exceptional. A moral shock might cause marked changes in the blood. After a great fright, a patient showed a drop in arterial pressure and a decrease in the number of white corpuscles.

"Thought can generate organic lesions," he writes. "The instability of modern life, the ceaseless agitation and the lack of security create states of consciousness which bring about nervous and organic diseases of the stomach and

2

intestines, defective nutrition and the passage of intestinal microbes into the circulatory apparatus.

"Colitis and the accompanying infections of the kidneys and of the bladder are the remote results of mental and moral unbalance. Such diseases are almost unknown in social groups where life is simpler and not too agitated, where anxiety is less constant. In a like manner, those who keep the peace of their inner self in the midst of the tumult of the modern city are immune from nervous and organic diseases."

Note the key words, *those who keep the peace of their inner self.*

We are all painfully familiar with the fact that anger will increase blood pressure. Bad news that causes a shock will make the blood drain away from the cheeks and can even make the hair turn white. Fear will produce numbness. Hatred and jealousy will poison the system as effectively as any harmful drug. Cheerfulness, optimism and confidence will increase health by stimulating the physical mechanism.

Many outstanding cures have been achieved wholly by concentrated will power. President Roosevelt was a supreme example of what determination can do. Instead of surrendering, he met the challenge of infantile paralysis and so triumphed over it that he successfully directed the affairs of the nation in the most critical years of American history.

The records of Christian Science reveal that many organic diseases have been cured purely by mental processes. Faith will cure these diseases, as the records at Lourdes testify. Even though the proportion of cures is not large compared with the number of pilgrims, the successes are verified by medical men before cures are accepted.

Scores of doctors have given their patients bottles of coloured water and these have resulted in cures simply because the sufferers believed that they were imbibing tonics with health-giving properties.

One doctor tells the story of a new injection for a gastric ulcer which he tried on a girl patient. She telephoned in great excitement three days after the first injection to announce that she had eaten solid foods which before she was unable to assimilate. An X-ray confirmed that the ulcer was diminishing in size. The doctor reported the results to the colleague who had sent him the ampoules containing the injection. "Good," said the colleague, "I had better send you another half a dozen doses."

"But I have still got six left," said the doctor.

When he made a check, he discovered that originally there had been six ampoules of powder and six of ordinary distilled water. He had injected the distilled water.

The relationship between mind and body is also seen in faith healing, which has resulted in cures in a large number of cases that were medically incurable. The Rev. John Maillard, the Church of England clergyman who founded the Sanctuary of Healing at Milton Abbey, Dorset, in 1936, became interested in faith healing when he was a boy. Because his mother was an invalid, he was allowed to see her only at specified times. One day, when he called, she was, at first, too ill to speak. He sat and held her hand.

When he rose to go, his mother asked if he had been praying for her. He said he had, but when he got outside he was horrified at the lie he had told. Yet from that moment his mother began to improve. Her faith in prayer which had not been offered was responsible for the change.

After being ordained, Maillard determined to devote himself to healing. Among his many subsequent cures was the man he went to see in hospital who was suffering with cancer in the mouth and throat. An incision had been made in the throat to enable the patient to breathe and to take liquid nourishment. After the clergyman's first visit, the man began to recover and ultimately made a complete recovery.

Godfrey Mowatt is another faith healer who works under the auspices of the Church of England. When he was seven, an accident with a penknife cost him the sight of one eye. Two years later, through another accident, he lost the sight of the other. He was in agony and lived in a world of self-pity, until he realised that he had to do something constructive with his life.

He discovered that sick people took a turn for the better when he was in their presence. He attributed these successes to the fact that he talked to them on religious matters and succeeded in removing their depression. "If you can bring peace to the mind, the body responds," he says.

As an example of what can be accomplished by faith healing, he tells of a visit to the Midlands to conduct healing services. When he arrived at one church, there was a woman walking up and down outside, very moved and hardly able to speak. She said that she had been crippled in her legs for years. On the previous evening, she had attended his faith-healing service at which she had to be helped to the altar. Now she had come to give thanks for her cure, which was evidenced by the fact that she had walked all the way from the station.

Another faith healer, the Rev. William Wood, an Anglican priest, maintains that all illnesses, functional, psychological and organic, have a spiritual background. He even asserts that infection from germs is far more liable if there is no spiritual health in a person. Whether you agree or not with his contentions, there are records at the London Healing Mission, where he works, to demonstrate that faith healing produces results after medicine has failed.

All these examples reveal the tremendous powers possessed by the mind and underline my thesis that you can enjoy full health if you are determined to have it. Positive thinking is creative, while fear and worry lead to illness and disease. You must remember that good health is normal and that disease is abnormal. When thinking and living are right, mind and body are working in harmony, with beneficial results to both.

CHAPTER IV

THE WILL TO LIVE

THE will to live has been a determining factor in the recovery of patients whose condition was regarded as hopeless, just as the will to die has defeated the greatest medical skill and attention.

Raimundo de Ovies, author and psychiatrist, describes how he cured himself of a grievous heart affection by sheer will power. "When I was ill," he writes, "I carried with me everywhere an ampoule of amyl nitrate. The seizure and the pain and characteristic dread led my physician to diagnose my case as angina pectoris. Then I decided I had the power to get well, so I dispensed with the ampoule and any concern over the heart condition. I paid no attention to the next seizure and it was brief. There was another that lasted only moments, but no third."

Thirty years after he was stricken with the heart trouble, he explained his cure as being due to giving his soul power to cure him while he

thought "only of the glory of life"—in other
words, his mind set into motion the power to
cure himself.

Even more outstanding is the case of Earl
Carlson, an American doctor, one of the world's
leading authorities on spastic children. These
are a pitiable sight, for they have no power to
control their limbs and have to face life as helpless cripples.

As a child, Carlson was a spastic, pronounced
incurable by doctors. Yet he cured himself, not
by any medical means, but by sheer determination. He describes the process in his book, *Born
That Way*. His account is an inspiration to all
who are stricken with illness. Sir Stafford Cripps
called it a book "of the most inspiring human
adventure." The Archbishop of Canterbury was
so impressed by it that it led him to accept the
Presidency of the British Council for the Welfare
of Spastics.

Carlson was born in America of poor parents.
His birth was a difficult one and the doctor had
to use forceps. The result was a grave injury to
the child's brain. Though his mental powers were
not affected, the boy had no co-ordination of
brain and muscle. If he wanted to move an arm
or leg, his brain was unable to transmit the
message to his limb. As a child, Carlson was

helpless. It was only with difficulty that he could drag himself along on crutches.

Then came the first remarkable happening. Whilst out in his pushcart one day, he was wheeled past a market stall and grabbed an apple. For the first time in his life, the child's arm and hand had performed a deliberate action. Later in life, Carlson realised what had happened. He had wanted the apple so badly that his brain had forced his limbs to function in order to satisfy his desire. It was a triumph of mind over matter.

The second astonishing incident occurred two years later. He was struggling along on his crutches when a team of horses bolted. The boy was so scared that he dropped his crutches and ran all the way home!

At the age of eight, Carlson began to attend school. His hard-working parents could not afford to supply him with transport. It was, therefore, difficult for him to make the journey. But because he *had* to do it, he *did* it. That was the start of a terrible struggle between mind and body. Slowly, by extraordinary self-discipline, he forced his muscles to obey him.

He won a scholarship to college, and as an undergraduate tasted alcohol for the first time. He found it gave him temporary control over his limbs, but when its effect wore off he was in just

2*

as bad a state as previously. Carlson realised the meaning of this occurrence, the alcohol removed self-consciousness. This induced him to start a campaign to instil self-confidence. He forced himself to do things that terrified him. He drove a car, went out alone in a canoe, and performed all kinds of actions that depended for their success upon his self-confidence.

It was hard going, but it worked. Carlson acquired faith in himself, and that, coupled with his desperate determination to make his muscles obey him, finally achieved a cure.

Dr. Arnold Hutschnecker has written a remarkable book, *The Will to Live*, in which, drawing on twenty-five years of medical experience, he cites many dramatic cases to prove that the state of health and even the span of life are controlled by the mind.

A very old woman, who had devoted her life to pioneering work in education, suffered from a dangerous illness in her middle years. While she lay hovering between life and death, she overheard two of her co-workers talking just outside her room in the hospital.

"If we could only reach her," said one, with passion in her voice, "if we could only make her understand how much we need her." These words, coming when her life lay in the balance, resurrected her will to live. They ended her wavering and gave her an incentive to pluck up courage and to resume the struggle. From that moment, her recovery began.

If you have something to live for, says this doctor, this will becomes a powerful force in combating illness. Medical men recognise this power when in a crisis of an illness they say, "We have done all we can; now it is up to the patient."

He instances the large number of sufferers who haunt doctors' surgeries and fail to obtain relief, no matter what treatment they receive. Their symptoms are many and varied, lack of sleep, pains in different parts of the body, nervousness and depression. One theme, however, is common to all of them. They complain of being unrelievedly tired. They speak with envy of those who appear to have boundless energy and who wake refreshed every morning. They say in sorrow that they wake more tired than when they went to bed.

The doctor contends that their energy has simply not disappeared, because it is a law of physics that no energy is lost. He asserts that the answer to their problem is that their energy is devoured by an inner struggle. The physician cannot help because they are in a state of mental

civil war, battling against rebellious forces within
themselves. Their sickness can be healed only
when the mind finds peace and its attention is
turned to something which its owner can pursue
with enthusiasm. Then weariness disappears.

Ordinary men and women can carry on heroic
exertions for long periods, with little rest and
without undue fatigue. In the prolonged air raids
over London in World War II, it was feared that
plague or epidemic would result in a population
living under this strain, with little sleep and
crowded in shelters every night. Yet Winston
Churchill stated: "The fact remains that during
this rough winter the health of the Londoners
was actually above the average. The power of
enduring suffering, when the spirit is aroused,
seems to have no bounds."

Dr. Alexis Carrell makes a similar point:
"Physical pain and hardship are easily supported
if they accompany the success of a cherished
enterprise. Death itself may smile when it is
associated with some great adventure, with the
beauty of sacrifice, or with the illumination of
the soul that becomes immersed in God."

The effects of long emotional stresses from
hidden conflicts are highly destructive, says Dr.
Hutschnecker. When the emotional stress is
relieved and the patient has the will to live,

"miracles" of healing may occur which are difficult to explain by biological medicine alone.

Fear is capable of lowering resistance to illness, another indication of the close connection between mind and body. Some years ago, a young man came to this same medical man and asked to be examined for polio. As the patient showed no symptoms of it, the doctor was obliged to tell him that they knew of no way to test susceptibility to the disease which his visitor feared. The following year, the young man went to another physician, with a similar demand to be examined for polio. Again he was reassured that he did not have the disease. The third year, however, he contracted an acute case of polio.

Dr. Hutschnecker maintains that premature signs of age, such as stooping and a shambling walk, are proof that the mind has wearied too soon of the struggle of life. "We age not by years but by our emotional reactions to events," he says. One man might lose his money and become grey overnight. Another will suffer reverses, struggle for a period and then find a new direction and forge ahead once more. He might show the scars of his bout with adversity by a few new lines in his face, but he has refused to submit to the tryanny of the calendar, as too many people do. Instead, he has exerted himself, made new creative efforts and is keeping himself young.

So potent is the mind, says the doctor, that when you say of a colleague, "He makes me sick," you often mean it literally. You become conscious of growing nausea, or the stab of pain, or the throbbing which precedes a headache. It is not the colleague but your own emotional response to him that is the cause of the indigestion or migraine. The physical pain you feel is just as real as laughter when you are amused, or tears when you are sad.

You can learn to change these emotional responses by mental determination. You have two courses from which to choose, fight or flight. Once you determine to fight, you are on the road back to health.

Says the doctor, "When you come out at the wrong end of an interview because fear has kept you from fighting back, your frustration and suppressed rage may give you a splitting headache by the end of the day. Conversely, if you cast aside your fears and act positively, the effect may prove highly exhilarating."

He gives a striking example of the relationship between mind and body in the story of a young dentist who complained that he was unhappy in his work as an assistant in a large fashionable practice composed of wealthy patients. He was troubled by his gall bladder and was subject to attacks of dizziness and fainting. Obviously, he could not continue in a work which he disliked so much that it was making him ill. He wanted to be a writer, but there was an economic problem. He had a wife and young child to support.

The doctor suggested that he should try to find more congenial work. The young dentist moved his family to a small town where the cost of living was much lower than in the metropolis. He lived in a tiny house that was almost bare, keeping limited hours for patients and earned just enough to pay his way. The rest of his time he devoted to writing. His first novel had a good reception and his second was sold to a reputable publisher. The young man was in no way troubled by the austerity of his life, for it brought him happiness and, above all, health. There was no recurrence of the complaints which had previously troubled him.

Dr. Hutschnecker contends that most people rarely achieve the best of which they are capable, largely because they ignore their hidden forces. The will is so powerful a force that many think it can take care of itself, but it has to be cultivated and fostered. It could be weakened and destroyed, as was proved by the number of people who died before their time, or who lived on half their mental capacity.

The body may age in later life, but a mind which is used properly need never age at all. Mental and physical age do not advance at the same rate. There are old minds in young bodies and young minds in old bodies. People who have the idea that learning stops with the end of school life are inviting old age.

The doctor writes: "When we stop learning, we begin to grow old. When we stop being interested, we begin to grow old. When we stop using our bodies, we begin to grow old. There is no physiological age at which we must stop all activity. Hence there is no age at which we must grow old." He repeats the excellent adage of another doctor, "The problem is not to add years to our life but to add life to our years."

In this connection, it is worth quoting the view of Dr. Alexis Carrell that the diseases of the mind are a serious menace and more dangerous than tuberculosis, cancer, heart and kidney diseases and even typhus, plague and cholera. The potency of the mind is revealed in grief. To a woman, the loss of her child can cause greater suffering than the loss of a limb. The breaking of an affectionate bond may even bring about death.

CHAPTER V

"MAN, KNOW THYSELF"

THE will to live is the result of many factors, and not all of them are conscious. Pschologists have a favourite illustration; they liken the mind to an iceberg, nine-tenths of which is under water. The tenth is your conscious aspect and the rest is your subconscious mind.

The power of the subconsciousness has been utilised to obtain cures. Coué demonstrated that by instilling into it the resolute determination, "Every day, in every way, I am getting better and better," beneficial physical results were achieved.

Hypnotism enables the subconscious mind to work in a similar fashion. Susceptible subjects (and these are always people with positive and not negative personalities because then there is something to hypnotise) have been enabled to cure themselves of all manner of diseases. Many medical men now resort to hypnotic treatment when normal methods have failed.

In post-hypnotic experiments, suggestions made while subjects are, to all intents and purposes, fast asleep, are acted upon at the precise time previously indicated. The psychiatrist, by liberating hidden fears, sometimes from childhood days, utilises the potency of the mind to achieve results which illustrate the interaction of mind and body.

The truth is that the body is a self-healing organism. It will always seek to eliminate the causes of illnesses. Properly directed mental efforts will hasten the natural processes of recuperation. Startling results are being obtained simply by teaching patients how to relax properly, a difficult process which calls for a combination of mental and physical quiescence.

The body is the most wonderful example of a co-ordinated, complex mechanism, completely renewing itself, and performing a thousand and one delicate operations every moment of our lives. Take one small example. No machine ever built by human beings can compare in ingenuity or efficiency with ordinary muscle. Almost every movement in life is controlled by the power of the muscles. Somehow or other, the soft jelly-like muscle tissue is able to harden and contract in such a manner that it can lift a thousand times its own weight. And it can do so hundreds of times a second if necessary.

The human body is extremely robust. It

adapts itself to all climatic conditions ranging from tropical heat to arctic cold. It will resist starvation, the vagaries of the weather, overwork, weariness and hardship. Of all the animals man is the hardiest. Resistance to disease, work and worries, capacity of effort, and nervous equilibrium are signs of man's superiority.

Says Dr. Alexis Carrell: "There is a striking contrast between the durability of our body and the transitory character of its elements. Man is composed of a soft, alterable matter, susceptible of disintegrating in a few hours. However, he lasts longer than if made of steel. Not only does he last, but he ceaselessly overcomes the difficulties and dangers of the outside world. He accommodates himself, much better than the other animals do, to the changing conditions of his environment. He persists in living, despite physical, economic and social upheavals. The body seems to mould itself on events. Instead of wearing out, it changes. Our organs always improvise means of meeting every new situation."

When you consider the ceaseless activity concealed beneath our skins and the stresses to which the body is subjected through ignorance of nature's laws, the marvel is that we do not get more trouble.

From the moment of an injury to the body, the

processes of self-healing begin to work. Highly skilful surgeons have admitted that their efforts are amateurish compared with those nature performs in the millions of operations which are matters of course in bodily activities. Doctors get credit for cures that are due entirely to nature. The wise physician realises that all his efforts must be directed to co-operating with the body's inherent self-healing.

"Indeed, as every doctor knows," writes Kenneth Walker, a Harley Street specialist, in *Diagnosis of Man*, "all that he does is to act in the capacity of nature's humble and admiring assistant." Sometimes the body has to perform its tasks despite the labours of uninformed medical men whose prescriptions ignore the vital facts of nature's healing.

Dr. Carrell has instanced what happens when skin, muscles, blood vessels or bones are injured. "The organism immediately adapts itself to such a new situation," he writes. "Everything happens as if a series of measures, some immediate, some delayed, were taken by the body in order to repair the lesions of the tissues. They all tend towards the end to be attained, the reconstruction of the destroyed structures."

He describes what occurs when an artery is cut. The blood gushes in abundance. Pressure on the artery is lowered. Respiration and circulation are temporarily suspended. The hæmorrhage lessens and a clot forms in the wound. A curdled substance closes the opening of the vessel. Then the hæmorrhage definitely stops. During the following days, white blood corpuscles and tissues cells invade the clot and progressively regenerate the wall of the artery.

Each tissue, he says, is capable of responding, at any moment of the unpredictable future, to all physical and chemical changes in a manner consistent with the interests of the whole body. "Individual cells appear to act in the interest of the whole," he writes, "just as bees work for the good of the hive. They seem to know the future. And they prepare for this future by anticipated changes of their structure and functions."

Modern surgery had been brought into being by the knowledge of the processes of self-healing, he states. Surgeons would not be able to treat wounds if bodily adaptation did not exist. They have no influence on the healing mechanisms. They content themselves with guiding the spontaneous activity of those mechanisms.

"For example," he adds, "they manage to bring the edges of a wound, or the ends of a broken bone, into such a position that regeneration takes place without defective scar or deformity. In order to open a deep abscess, treat an infected fracture, perform a Cæsarean operation, extirpate a portion of the stomach or of the intestines, or raise the roof of the skull and remove a tumour from the brain, they have to make long incisions and extensive wounds. The most accurate sutures would not suffice definitely to close such openings if the organism were not capable of making its own repairs. Surgery is based on the existence of this phenomenon."

This wonderful bodily mechanism, with all its self-healing properties, is at your command, if you determine to take charge, as you were intended. You have the power to do so.

All our intricate, unceasing bodily activity begins with cells that are microscopically minute. What a silent but profound tribute to the Infinite Intelligence which is responsible! And what a salutary lesson for science, which can manufacture atomic bombs but cannot make a piece of skin, a fingernail, or one tiny hair!

Life eludes the scientist. He cannot create it. He cannot subject it to analysis in a laboratory. Though the constituents of the human body are known, no one can create a living organism.

Death occurs because mind and consciousness have departed. That is why the heart ceases to beat, the blood to circulate and the lungs no longer operate. The driving power and the engineer have gone. It is mind which directs the body, even though many instructions are given subconsciously. The body is the servant of the mind.

Marvellous though the body is, it cannot match the wonder of the mind. The body exists because of the mind and spirit. Where there is conscious, individual life, mind and spirit have been at work, moulding the body for their purpose. Mind and spirit are the eternal realities on which our bodies depend for their existence.

Modern scientific research demonstrates that the basis of matter is in the invisible. Science today reads almost like a fairy tale. In its materialistic beginning it denied the reality of anything that could not be measured by the five senses. Its own progress, if that is the right word to apply to some of its awesome discoveries and inventions, is responsible for exploding the materialistic concept of life. One day, even science may reveal that matter owes its existence to spirit.

The fact of your birth gives you a divine heritage. You are spirit. "God is spirit," says the Bible and you are God in miniature. In embryonic form, you possess all the divine attributes. You share in the processes of eternal creation. Within you is part of the power that fashioned the majestic universe in all its multitudinous manifestations.

You are not a worm wriggling in the dust of obscurity. You are not a body that will decay and join the elements which compose it. This is what the ancients meant when they asserted, "Man, know thyself." This is what is meant by the sublime declaration, "The kingdom of heaven is within."

You have not scratched the surface of the rich treasures awaiting your excavation. Life, properly understood and directed, is a tremendous and exhilarating adventure in which you develop all your innate gifts and faculties.

Within you is the power to overcome all obstacles. You can unfold and express latent forces that will bring you into touch with the infinite storehouse. Man has never been comprehended in his entirety. He contains vast unexplored territories. His potentialities are well nigh inexhaustible.

The body is important because it is the temple of the mind and spirit. The temple must be a fitting habitation. The body was not intended to live in squalor and slumdom, to be riddled with disease, to be clad in rags, or to lack the warmth, food and shelter necessary for its highest development. You are not fulfilling your divine destiny if you live in the darkness, physical, mental or spiritual, instead of the light.

You must learn to live rightly on all planes of activity. Just as the mind moulds the body for its purpose, you can mould circumstances to achieve your birthright. Those who succumb and admit defeat are denying their own heritage. Both within and without are the means by which victory can be achieved.

CHAPTER VI

". . . TAKEN AT THE FLOOD"

"There is a tide in the affairs of men, which, taken at the flood, leads on to fortune."

FOR a quarter of a century, his brilliant advocacy in the courts earned for Sir Patrick Hastings about £25,000 a year. Yet when he came home from the South African war, he had hardly a penny to his name. He climbed the ladder of fame and fortune unaided by family backing, influential friends or by money. He rose to the top of his chosen profession and earned by his one-man industry the vast sum of £625,000 in twenty-five years.

How did Sir Patrick achieve this transformation from poverty to wealth? It was done by following a formula which he outlined in these words: "A long experience has satisfied me beyond question that *there is no reasonable objective which any man of ordinary intelligence cannot achieve, provided he really wants it and really means to achieve it.* At least ninety per cent. of

the failures in life are people who either don't
want anything very much or, if they do, don't
really try very hard to get it."

You might say that this is a simple formula.
It is, but to keep to it demanded qualities of
character, endurance and determination that
were proof against the difficulties and despair
which others do not overcome. In Sir Patrick's
case, the obstacles could have been regarded as
formidable. At twenty-one, he had no home and
so little money that he pawned his war medal for
two shillings and sixpence in order to buy
food.

"As I had no money," he said, "I had all the
necessary incentive to make some. And if a
young man is unable to keep himself, he is probably not very well worth keeping."

He was faced with the problem of maintaining
himself and of acquiring, in three years, the
knowledge and the hundred pounds needed to be
called to the Bar. This is how he solved his
problems. He took three temporary jobs at the
same time and went without lunch on most
working days. Every day, he walked a distance
of eight miles from his suburban home to the
West End of London. This took him two hours.
He walked home again in the middle of the night,
arriving frequently at three in the morning. In

every spare moment he studied as hard as he could.

His shabbiness gave him some bad moments, when he doubted the likelihood of achieving his goal, but he soon overcame despondency and determined never to give in. He said, "The money came very slowly, but there are always twenty-four hours in a day—and at a pinch they can be turned into twenty-five."

In the first year, he saved twenty pounds, in the second, forty pounds and he reached the hundred pounds' mark a fortnight before he was called to the Bar. Later, money came easily. His attitude to it was: "Money is quite a good thing to work for, especially if it is to be spent on somebody else, but it is not much good to anybody who does not have to work for it."

He never lost his zest for life and declared that he could not recall one moment when he was bored. His own words are, "I cannot remember one day which was not tinged with some element of adventure, either of hope or disappointment, of failure or achievement."

Sir Patrick had found the secret of success. Mark well his words, *"There is no reasonable objective which any man of ordinary intelligence cannot achieve, provided he really wants it and really means to achieve it."*

I read with interest, the other day, a newspaper account which referred to a man as "Mr. Success." The key words were, "His determination never faltered." It was the story of a young man who worked the lift in a London newspaper office. "Sometimes," added the account, "he carried cups of tea instead. But always he determined that these tasks were paving stones to success. *His determination never faltered.*"

After working the lift for three years, he left the London office for a job in the provinces. One day, he raised the money to buy a weekly newspaper that was losing three thousand pounds a year. After two years, it was making a net profit of fifteen hundred pounds a year. His determination had produced results.

As you can see, it is the attitude of mind that is all important. Take the case of Jack Hylton, now one of our great impresarios, who began in humble circumstances. His father worked as a twister in a cotton mill.

Explaining how his philosophy originated with his father's attitude, Hylton says: "In all his life, I never knew him to worry about money, *not even when he had it*. He wanted money, of course. Like most Lancashiremen, he wanted to look after himself. But he was sure that he could. So he did not worry."

His father could afford little schooling for young Hylton. To make certain that in time his son could stand on his own feet, the father sat by him for hours on end, making him practise the piano until he was good enough to accompany his parent's songs on Saturday nights in the public house which he later owned.

Hylton says: "I made more money than my dad did. I've also lost more. The money I've got now is all invested in various shows and copyrights, and a run of failures could put me on my back. But I don't worry. I know I could get up again."

He refused to worry when his voice broke and ended his Lancashire music-hall career as the Singing Mill Boy. He began a new career as an accompanist to singers in public houses and on the sands in a North Wales town. Though he had never conducted before, when he was seventeen he managed to secure an engagement at thirty-five shillings a week as a touring pantomime conductor.

When a concert party became bankrupt he did not worry. Hylton took on the management and was still not worrying when, after paying all the debts, he found that he had not a penny left for a cup of tea on the train returning to London!

Young Hylton returned to concert party after the first world war when he did a double act with Tommy Handley. Strange to relate, they were a failure. Hylton went on to play the piano in a night club and to plug songs on the sands at Blackpool.

Then the wheel of fortune turned. He happened to hear the first Paul Whiteman record brought to this country. This made him realise that the music which Whiteman played was properly orchestrated, instead of being the usual haphazard improvisations. He started to orchestrate music for an English band. The recordings they made were an immediate success.

When, however, he asked the members of the band to pay him ten shillings each from the fees they received from the recording companies as payment for his orchestrations, they objected and unanimously decided to dispense with his services. But the recording companies still wanted his services for orchestration, and that was the beginning of the famous Jack Hylton orchestra.

At the beginning of the second world war, he went into management at one of London's leading West End theatres. He is often asked, he says, whether he gets cold feet before the curtain goes up on a new production, because of the large amount of money at stake. He answers that this thought never occurs to him. There are so many problems running through his mind at the time that the money element really does not enter into it.

It becomes a consideration only later when the new venture is either a success or a failure. If it is a success, then the money involved does not matter so much. If it is a failure, he does not worry, but faces the situation logically. Does he take the play off, or continue it in the hope that results may improve? More often than not, he says he starts to plan for another production straight away, which may or may not be successful.

Hylton is an example of a man with a single purpose, one who realises that worry is worthless. Whatever you desire must begin in your mind. The first steps to success are determination, will power and resolution. Every circumstance must be regarded as a stepping stone. You must see the goal in your mind, where you must always regard it as having been reached. Your attitude must be that on the mental plane your aim has been achieved. You must refuse to recognise that obstacles can stand in the way.

A friend of mine, a gifted natural healer, was besieged by sufferers when the news travelled that he had cured his wife of cancer after she was given only six weeks to live. In his small flat, he could not cope with all the requests for healing. He loved to walk on a nearby common and was always drawn to an attractive piece of land adjoining it. He realised that it would make an ideal site on which to build a healing sanctuary and he was determined to have it.

Each day, on his walk, he visited the land. Mentally he built a wall around it for himself. He visualised his new sanctuary operating from that site. He planned the entrance, the healing quarters, the living accommodation and the garden. From the standpoint of will, it was *his* property. When he visited the local estate agents, they told him the land was not for sale, and the owner had no desire to build on it. The healer was not dismayed.

He went to see the owner, who at first would not entertain the idea of selling his land. My friend wore him down and made him enthusiastic at the idea of his property being used to heal the sick. The owner was now willing to sell, but there was one great obstacle. His mother, who lived close to the site, would certainly object to a healing sanctuary because the numerous patients constantly coming and going would disturb her peace.

3

The healer went for his usual daily walk and performed his regular concentration on the piece of land. His resolve never faltered. He made an appointment to see the mother. When he arrived and told her the object of his call, he was met with an immediate refusal. But he persisted until he won her over. She became so keen that she insisted on presenting some chairs to the sanctuary. For many years, thousands of sick people were successfully treated in the building which was erected just as the healer had visualised it when he resolved that the site was ideal for his purpose.

You must have your objective firmly fixed in your mind before it can be realised. This must be a positive resolution, with no doubts being admitted. You must persist, day after day, and night after night, concentrating on your objective. You must visualise it, regard it as mentally achieved and determine to make it materialise. Draw a mental ring round it and "pull" it towards you.

Before you go to sleep each night "tune in" to the power within and without. Achieve mental unity with all the creative forces of which you are a focal point. Express your unhesitating confidence that you will achieve your objective.

When you are completely convinced that success will be yours, and your faith is adamant, the result will come. Nothing can stop it. You have set in motion the means by which it will happen. You have placed yourself in the position to receive what you desire. You have "turned on the switch."

The constant mental repetition of the achievement required also has the effect of instilling this desire into your subconsciousness, which harnesses its potentialities for the accomplishment of the task. Like many other duties assigned to the subconscious mind, it becomes part of its routine. It searches into the depths of your being to stimulate into activity the reserve that is seldom used except in times of crisis. We are all familiar with the fact than in an emergency we tap a latent strength. This reserve is waiting to be utilised.

Always surround yourself with hope and optimism, for these are part of your essential equipment. They are vital elements in your mental outlook because they constitute a positive attitude towards life. They help to bring about the results you desire. When you are confident of success, you are on the way to achieve it. Think of yourself as a transmitting and receiving station. When you broadcast hope, faith and confidence, the atmosphere around you becomes bright, alert, alive and magnetic. Automatically you attract similar conditions and create the means by which the results must come.

CHAPTER VII

FEAR IS FUTILE

ONE who is familiar with the higher truths has put on record the experience that changed his outlook. He writes: "For forty years I was afflicted with some of the most horrible diseases known to mankind. How I suffered with them! Worse than cancer, worse than polio, worse than angina, the diseases which came upon me made my life a hell on earth.

"The first disease was a severe case of pessimism. If there was the slightest tinge of darkness in connection with anything, I managed, no matter how difficult it was, to find that darkness.

"Another disease was false desires. How I yearned to have possessions which would not have been good for me! How I longed to do things which would have brought me (and often did) pangs of regret! I charged down the road after a fleeing and fleeting happiness, and I always came to the end of the road to find that I had been shadow-chasing again.

"Envy was a curious sort of ulcer that gnawed at my insides till I could hardly stand the pain.

I was always hoping someone would die and leave me some wonderful inheritance. The companion disease, of course, is selfishness. These two nearly always make their appearance together. They enjoy each other's company, but you will not find them enjoyable guests."

Finally he went to a doctor, who made an X-ray examination of the stomach. This showed that he had an ulcer. The doctor said that he would have to ease up and stop worrying.

"That night I got thinking," says the writer. "I decided, 'This doctor doesn't know all about me. He thinks I worry, and really I don't, but I do have a lot of other diseases. They are just too many to try and cure. I think I will die instead.'

"So I got out paper and pencil. 'If I am going to die,' I told myself, 'I am going to make a will.' I made a list of all my possessions, not my house and my car and my money. Those are just things that I am using. The things I had and owned are the things I put down. Here are some of them, envy, jealousy, pessimism, false desires, worry, fear, greed, selfishness.

"I 'died' the minute I signed that will. And no sooner did I 'die' than I received a wonderful inheritance from myself. I received cheerfulness, love, courage, generosity, justice, tolerance, ability, mental and spiritual prosperity and I think some material prosperity too. I received such a large inheritance that I cannot list it all.

"I went back to that doctor about six weeks later. He took another X-ray. I sat with him in his office when the nurse brought it in for him to see. He held it up to the light and a puzzled look came on his face. He took the card with my name on it from his file and tore it up. He did not have to tell me the ulcer was gone. Yes, I died ten years ago, and how glad I am to be alive today."

Fear and pessimism are both negative and destructive. They make the atmosphere around you listless, apathetic, heavy and dull. They block the channels by which help can come to you. You live in an aura of gloom. You attract forces which, by their very nature can only increase your despondency. Your mind, because it is wavering, ceases to be receptive to constructive ideas. "No man has failed unless he has lost the will to try again," was the motto of Teddy O'Neill, who pioneered a new form of education in Britain. The brave man is the one who conquers fear and then performs a heroic deed, not the individual who feels no fear at all.

Fear and worry are always your worst enemies. What a tonic President Roosevelt gave to his listening millions when he broadcast the simple but stirring declaration, "We have nothing to fear but fear." He knew that fear was corrosive and that worry warped the judgment.

Fear is futile. The individual who fears what the morrow will bring is helping to bring tomorrow's difficulties to him. When you worry you do not improve yourself or your lot. All you do is to make it impossible to think clearly and constructively. When your mind is filled with black despair, you have defeated yourself before you begin to fight. You can be concerned without worrying or indulging in fearful anxiety that makes your mind a hopeless blank.

There is no difficulty so strong that it is beyond your powers to overcome it, no load so heavy that your shoulders cannot bear it. Consider the grievous handicaps that others have conquered. Beethoven was stone deaf, Milton was blind, Pasteur was paralysed and Helen Keller suffered from blindness and deafness. Yet she was able to assert, "I thank God for my handicaps, for through them I have found myself, my work and my God." Why, then, should you be chained by fear?

Some people argue that they were born with a certain temperament and they cannot change it. If they believe they cannot, they certainly will not. If they believe they can, they will. Others blame their parents, or their environment.

Every child has in addition to all the usual physical factors contributed by his forbears his own X, the divine spark, the "unknown quantity," which is his own contribution to his evolution. His parents supply his body and his early environment, but they do not provide the X, the most vital asset.

History is full of examples of men and women, born of humble parents, in obscure surroundings, who have achieved greatness. Genius has been reared in circumstances that seemed completely alien to its flowering. Abraham Lincoln, who had less than twelve months' schooling, suffered unemployment, was in disgrace when he joined the army, and failed again and again, became the greatest President of the United States.

Moaning, groaning, bewailing and complaining will not enhance your position or your prospects. The man who is always looking for trouble will find it. Difficulties must be regarded as challenges which can and will be met, leaving you the stronger for having encountered them. You must make stepping stones of adversity, perplexity and frustration.

I saw in a newspaper a letter from a woman who wrote: "My husband has lost the use of his hands and has been given up as incurable by medical science. Can any reader suggest some

3*

ways or means whereby a man can earn a living, to make him feel he is still of some use in the world?"

One reply came from a man who said: "I too have lost the use of my hands, also my arms, legs and body. I can move only my head, neck and shoulders. I consider myself far from being helpless and useless. I pass my days reading, sketching and writing with pen or pencil in my mouth, and singing. Eventually, I hope to utilise at least one of these accomplishments to earn my living."

There was a light-hearted postscript, "I bet this is the first letter that has come to you 'by word of mouth.'"

A journalist who called reported that the man's writing was clearer and much better formed than her own. His drawings of landscapes and copies of portraits had to be seen to be believed, she added. Though for ten years he had been stricken with polio, he refused to give in or complain. Every Wednesday evening, smartly dressed and strapped in his wheel chair, he went to singing lessons, preparing for the day when he could professionally use his voice.

An even more astonishing demonstration of the determination to defeat disability is the case of Miss Anine Tellefsen, a Norwegian woman who recently celebrated her seventieth birthday.

When she was fifteen, she contracted tuberculosis so severely that in three years she had to undergo four operations, the last being for the amputation of her two arms. Four years later, she was confronted with the terrible verdict that both her legs would also have to be amputated. Thus, while still in her twenties, she faced life without legs and arms.

Miss Tellefsen made up her mind that, so far as was possible, she would not be a burden on anyone else. She decided that she had to earn her own living. After contemplating the very restricted means of employment available to her, she concluded that she must learn to sew with her mouth.

At the hospital she had already learned to write with her mouth. Now she began the arduous task of producing embroidery and fine lace, with all the sewing done by her mouth. Her first results were sold at a bazaar and realised sufficient money to support her for some years.

It is difficult enough to thread the tiny eye of a needle even with both hands, but after years of practice Miss Tellefsen has succeeded in accomplishing this task with ability and agility. First, the needle is placed vertically on a cushion on a table. Then she takes a pair of scissors in her mouth and, with these, she grips the thread, aiming so accurately that she is able to slip it through the eye.

When doing embroidery, she puts the needle on the line of the pattern. She gives the needle a push with her shoulder, and pulls it out again with her mouth. To keep her shoulders in position for the task, she has them strapped.

On her seventieth birthday she received a gold medal from the King, who, in granting her an audience, wanted a detailed account of how she managed to do her beautiful work. He congratulated her on the unique good humour which never fails her.

She insists that life has been good, although she has been without arms and legs for fifty years. Her work has been a great help in her extreme disability and has prevented her from being depressed and miserable. The feeling that she can earn her own living has been of great importance. All her work is sold by means of raffles in her town and they now fetch a high price.

Miss Tellefsen is able to walk by means of artificial legs attached to her stumps. She lives in Langesund, her native town, where she has a little flat with a housekeeper who helps her to dress and gives her meals.

This cripple is a devout woman, and has sung for several years in a church choir. She has now been chosen as a representative on a committee for the disabled, so that she can help to improve the legislation for those unable to earn their own living because they are maimed.

A newspaper reporter who interviewed her, described her as an ideal woman, happy in her outlook and forthright in her utterances.

You must remember that there are many causes for the weakening of the body. It is well known that the quality of its tissues is lowered by too poor or too rich a diet, by excessive alcohol and also by prosperity and leisure. While civilised men degenerate in tropical climates, they thrive in temperate or cold countries. Man needs a way of life involving constant struggle, mental and muscular effort, physical, mental and moral discipline and some privations.

These conditions innure the body to fatigue and to troubles. They protect it against disease, especially nervous diseases. They irresistibly drive man to conquer the world in which he lives.

Dr. Alexis Carrell has observed: "Man attains his highest development when he is exposed to the rigours of the seasons, when he sometimes goes without sleep, sometimes sleeps for long hours, when his meals are sometimes abundant and sometimes scanty, when he conquers food and shelter at the price of strenuous efforts. He has also to train his muscles, to tire himself and rest, to fight, suffer and be happy. His will needs alternately to strain and to relax. He is made for such an existence, just as the stomach is made for digesting food. When his adaptive processes work most intensely, he develops his virility to the fullest extent. Hardships make for nervous resistance and health.''

The truth is that problems are good for us. They are the means by which character is developed. Without them, the human race would become spineless. Gold emerges only after the dirty yellow ore had been crushed, refined purified. Your real self often does not emerge until trouble has touched your soul.

Suffering and pain cease to be mysteries when they lead you to the deepest and highest aspects of your own being, making you aware of innate qualities whose existence you had never before realised. Thousands have found God, and found themselves, when life seemed to be in the shadows. It is part of the divine compensation that through the greatest suffering you attain the greatest knowledge.

Life is comparative. You enjoy sunshine only because you have dwelt in the shadows. You cannot appreciate wealth unless you have tasted poverty. Good health is not valued until you have experienced illness. It is because we have endured the horrors of war that we can enjoy the benefits of peace.

For some years, I corresponded with a friend in Jamaica who decided to pay his first visit to London. He was as brown as a berry, tanned by the sun, when he arrived in a chill November fog. How he revelled in that fog! Whereas I expected him to be disappointed he found it exhilarating. He explained that having sunshine day after day, for months on end, was a palling experience. The fog was a wonderful relief.

You get a different perspective of life when you are in an aeroplane. As you fly over cities and countries, your mind seems to detach itself from the trivialities, worries and meannesses of life on the ground. A sense of loftiness fills you. You enjoy a greater freedom. There are no hedges, barriers or frontiers to separate you from the other individuals. Your mind, too, has been given wings. The land over which you travel may be in shadow because of clouds which obscure the sun. But you are flying above those clouds and the sun is friendly and warm.

You watch the slowly moving clouds and see a rift. You know, though the people below you do not, that through the rift the rays of the sun will shine. They cannot see the light which you know will soon bring illumination to them. Because of your new horizon, you have a realisation and foresight which they do not possess.

Knowledge of life's greater realities will bring a similar change in your perspective. And fear will never find a resting place in your mind.

CHAPTER VIII

"THE FAULT, DEAR BRUTUS . . ."

NO matter how lowly your circumstances, so correspondingly high can you rise. Do not accept any barrier as a permanency. Do the best at the task to which you are assigned, even if you are dissatisfied with it, but tell yourself it is only a stepping stone because of your determination to succeed.

Correct thinking will bring a correct perspective. Your will power is an essential factor in determining your future. Professor J. B. Rhine, of Duke University, North Carolina, U.S.A., has performed, during the past few years, thousands of experiments which prove that the throws of dice can be willed and that results were obtained which could not be explained by chance.

The extent to which mind influences matter is still unknown. But it does exert a tremendous influence because mind is the controlling force. "The fault, dear Brutus, is not in our stars, but in ourselves, that we are underlings." That is the truth, but how many are prepared to face it?

Within yourself lies the explanation for all that has happened, is happening and will happen in your life. Do not blame others, or adverse circumstance. Do not rail at fate; blame yourself.

> *"It matters not how strait the gate,*
> *How charged with punishment the scroll,*
> *I am the master of my fate;*
> *I am the captain of my soul."*

Whatever the outside influences exerted on your life, within you is the power to overcome them all. "The child is the repository of infinite possibility," wisely said Andrew Jackson Davis, the "Seer of Poughkeepsie."

You may ask, "What about luck, chance, fate, free will and destiny?" Each plays its part in life, but none is stronger than your X, your unknown quantity, which enables you to be the master of your fate and the captain of your soul.

Besides, destiny may have a task for you to perform. Just before the election which was to make him Prime Minister again, Winston Churchill, probably the greatest man alive in the world to-day, was talking to a companion about his racehorse Colonist the Second. This animal, which had won more than ten times his purchase price, had a serious injury which ended his lucrative career.

Philosophically, Churchill said that perhaps he should not be disappointed. The hand of God might be behind it. He had been given this fascinating toy to play with at a time when he needed cheering. "If it has been taken from me now," he said, "it may be because the Almighty has more important things for me to do."

"This simple fatalism," says a close friend, "is a strong and touching trait in Churchill's character."

Natural law reigns throughout the whole universe; there is no effect without a cause. Philosophers have argued for centuries about fate and free will. Both may be true in the sense that some events are fated and that you have a limited free will. After all, an unrestricted free will is impossible in a universe ruled by natural law. In some cases, you can certainly make a choice, but it is dependent on your growth, character and the ruling circumstances.

You cannot control the laws of nature, but you can control the development of your mind, which is bound to affect your free will. It may be that life follows a rhythmic pattern in that there are cycles of good and bad luck—perhaps this is another way of saying that sometimes you are in harmony with the plan and sometimes you are not.

This does not affect my main contention, that by calling on your latent powers you can attain the goal of your achievement. Planets may influence your physical nature; palmistry may reveal crises that will occur in the future; phrenology may indicate faculties that can be developed; but none of these can prevent you from fulfilling your desires if you are determined to assert your innate superiority.

You can obtain all that you want, until you realise it is foolish to seek more than you need. "The saints are the richest people, because they want nothing," writes St. John Ervine in one of his plays. The mere piling up of wealth for wealth's sake, or for purely selfish reasons, will not help the development of your soul, which is the real reason for your life on earth. You can eat only one meal at a time, sleep in one bed at a time, or drive one car at a time.

It is no part of the divine plan that any individual should possess more than he needs. Moth and rust are divine safeguards, eternal reminders of the folly of selfish hoarding. Do not retain what you cannot use, or, in other words, "Lay not up for yourselves treasures upon earth,

where moth and rust doth corrupt, and where
thieves break through and steal."

Material security is virtually impossible, as
World War Two demonstrated. A bomb can
destroy your possessions and Acts of Parliament
affect the value of your properties. You must
make sure that your wealth does not own you,
that you become a miser, a mere slave to possessions.

All wealth is a stewardship. You are a trustee
who will have to account for the way you dis-
charged your responsibilities. "The earth is the
Lord's and the fullness thereof." Temporarily
you may be in charge of part of the fullness, but
it can never be yours for ever.

You have to die. It is the one factor that you
cannot evade. And you cannot determine when
the call will come. Those who commit suicide in
order to evade responsibility will find that they
have not cheated the natural laws.

With unconscious irony, a London evening
newspaper publishes details of wills under the
heading, "Money They Left." It has to be left
and, too often, it causes quarrels and dissensions.

It was revealed at the death of an American
multi-millionaire that many priceless acquisi-
tions, which his agents had bought on his behalf
all over the world, were still intact in their

packing cases. What a colossal waste! He had
not even derived the æsthetic pleasure of looking
at his beautiful possessions and he had prevented
others from feasting their eyes and minds on
them. Wealth cannot buy happiness; it can
only purchase pleasure. True happiness comes
from within.

The worship of wealth and the wealthy is a sad
commentary on mankind's sense of values. Richness of character is far more important than
money-bags. Many people desire wealth because
it brings power. So base and ignoble a motive
must react on the individual, impoverishing his
mind, spirit and character, which are his eternal
possessions.

Some amass fortunes by evading the laws of
their countries. They cannot, however, evade the
laws of God, which are the laws of nature. Effect
must follow cause, which is only another way of
saying that you must reap what you sow.

Once you understand the plan behind life, you
face each day with the confidence born of
knowledge. The infinite Power, which has made
provision for every facet of universal activity
through the operation of unfailing natural laws
which control, regulate and sustain them, has not
overlooked you. You cannot be forgotten or
neglected in the divine scheme.

Learn to live for the day. The past is gone; you cannot recall it. In vain are your regrets for what might have been. Bewailing lost opportunities will not improve your lot. Live for the day, and live in harmony with nature's laws, thus ensuring that tomorrow will bring you no misgivings.

Every new day provides you with the chance of making a fresh start. Know that your wants will be supplied, that no problem will arise which you cannot solve, no difficulty that you cannot conquer. Then yours will be an abundant life, full of exhilaration, with no fears to darken the horizon of your mind.

With head erect and shoulders squared, live for the day in the sunlit, radiant glory that is the lot of all who are in accord with the power behind life. Self-mastery is the greatest of all victories. Learn to stand on your own feet. If you do not expect anything from anybody, you cannot be disappointed.

When problems arise, as they must, do the best you can, for then your motive is right. And with the right motive, there will be no reproaches in later life. If, however, you allow your conduct to be guided by motives of expediency, you place yourself out of harmony with nature's laws, and you will have to pay the price.

If you are in real difficulty as to the right course to pursue, let your conscience, the divine monitor that each normal individual possesses, show you the way. The first answer, automatic in its response, is the path you should follow. Alas, too often, people attempt to still their conscience, to argue with it and to persuade themselves that they would be better off if they did not accept its clearly decisive verdict. And so selfishness triumphs and the divine prompting has been a wasted effort. The more you listen to the inner voice, the more you make yourself accessible to the guiding power that is within and without.

There is a rhythm in the universe exemplified in the pageant of the seasons, in the ebb and flow of the tides, in the rising and setting of the sun, in the ceaseless rotation of the earth, in the challenge of the morning and the peace of the night. Match the rhythm of your own being with nature's harmony, and the fullness of life will be yours for all time.

CHAPTER IX

HELP FROM THE UNSEEN

MAN is not alone in the universe. There is an invisible thread that binds him to every living creature. We are all members of one another. Our actions affect other members of the human family, just as their deeds, to a large or small extent, influence our lives. We cannot isolate ourselves from the rest of humanity. Our interdependence is a fact in nature from which, for good or ill, we cannot escape. In that sense, perhaps, we are our brothers' keepers.

How far do we affect one another in the mental and spiritual aspects of our being? Though the tie between us is invisible, it is none the less potent. We are all familiar with the experience of meeting people for the first time and, though they may not speak to us, we take an instant liking or dislike to them. Experience usually confirms the accuracy of our first impressions.

Many individuals radiate a warmth and magnetism that cannot be assessed in physical terms, yet these attributes are so real that we are immediately drawn to them. Then there are those who possess some natural healing faculty that sick people have only to be in their presence to feel beneficial results.

Every moment of the day, and often at night, we are receiving and transmitting invisible and inaudible vibrations, so far as our material senses are concerned. Telepathy reveals that distance is no barrier to mental communications. When it is operating successfully, it is just as easy to receive "messages" from another continent as from another room. There would seem to be some analogy with radio reception. It takes no longer to receive a radio message sent six thousand miles than it does at a distance of six feet. The fact that telepathy does occur is evidence of a tremendous reservoir of power that is tapped only on special occasions. Life would be transformed if it were regularly pressed into service.

It would put an end to deception. For *all* our thoughts would be known. The language barrier would be broken down and every member of the human family could communicate with everybody else. There would be no misunderstandings, deliberate or unintentional.

You must also recognise that mental and spiritual aid can reach you from minds beyond this world. Jacob's ladder, which depicted ascending and descending "angels," was more than a dream. On its infinite rungs, stretching from heaven to earth, there is a range of evolved beings, each greater than the one below. Because they are linked with one another, they provide access to the highest that you can reach. As you unfold, you make yourself receptive to higher influences. Your growth determines the peak of your attainment.

The fact of inspiration is evidence that man is helped from higher sources. Both here and hereafter, it is character which determines spiritual growth. The many reformers and pioneers, whose names are recorded with lustre in the pages of history because of their labours which improved the lot of humanity, do not lose the desire to serve because death has intervened. Life is a continuous and expanding process. Whatever qualities made people great here are continued elsewhere, and these qualities develop and become greater.

Those individuals, who have increased their lustre, are searching for receptive instruments to whom they can communicate their extended knowledge and power. Hence the many accounts in the Bible, and other sacred books, of prophets, seers and visionaries being guided from on high. Their contemporaries misunderstood the source of their inspiration and regarded with awe the results that seemed miracles to them. All that happened, however, was in accordance with natural law.

Evidence of inspiration and tapping the higher powers are not confined to ancient times; there are many striking examples in our own day. Take my friend, Harry Edwards, the famous spiritual healer, who has given public demonstrations in the largest halls of this land. His postbag averages nine thousand letters a week. Through his agency, thousands have been cured of "incurable" diseases. There are five hundred cures of cancer in his filing cabinets.

Many of these successes are obtained by what he calls absent healing, that is, intercession made for patients living at a distance, many of them overseas. Patient and healer have never met. Yet this higher power, with healing in its wings, will span oceans and continents and bring new life to despairing thousands.

Edwards is the first to admit that he does not heal. He is the instrument through whom the healing is performed. When he makes his intercession, he tunes in to the higher forces and makes himself at one with the unseen beings who use him as the instrument of their service.

When it comes to giving cases of inspiration

from the unseen, the testimony, both ancient and modern, is overwhelming. In his *Apology* Plato quotes Socrates as saying, "Not by wisdom do poets write poetry but by a sort of genius and inspiration."

Enid Blyton is the most prolific writer of children's stories in the world. She has twenty-four publishers, often writes ten thousand words a day, which earn for her around £50,000 a year, probably the highest income of any woman in Britain. She will open her portable typewriter at any time of the day and produce, without any hesitation, a new tale. She says that her mind is like a cinema screen on which the whole story is ready to be unfolded and all the characters, complete with their names, are waiting to depict the stirring adventures which delight thousands of children.

George Eliot volunteered that when she was writing certain dramatic scenes in *Middlemarch* she was "seized by a not-self."

When he read the proofs of one of his novels, Hugh Walpole declared, "I seemed to have had nothing to do with it."

Inspiration has a wide range. Edgar Wallace, famed for his thrillers, said that he never thought of plots; they came into his mind ready-made. "I start dictating my novels right away," he said, "and never think of the end. When I have been stuck for an idea and I have suddenly started again, my wife has asked, 'Why did you say, "Thank you"?' I have replied that I supposed I was thanking something and that I did not understand it."

Henry Arthur Jones confessed, "God seems to give me plots ready-made."

Sir Hall Caine dreamed the plot of *The Woman of Knockaloe* three times in one night and knew that he had to write it. The plot of *Dr. Jekyll and Mr. Hyde* came to Robert Louis Stevenson in a dream. Parts of *Kubla Khan* were dreamed by Coleridge.

The famous hymn, *O Love that wilt not let me go*, was the result of a burst of inspiration. Its author, Dr. George Matheson, said: "It was composed with extreme rapidity; it seemed to me that its construction occupied only a few minutes, and I felt myself rather in the position of one who was being dictated to than of an original artist."

A modern poet, Frederic Irving Taylor, describes the process of inspiration in these words: "Judging by my own experiences, some of one's finest lines seem to lilt themselves while the poet is in a sort of rapture or reverie, as if such lines, at any rate, were projected into consciousness by some unseen personality comparable with the Muse of the Ancients.

"Upon surveying the vista of inspiration thus mysteriously poured into the brain like a sunburst, and thereupon deciding to carry out the work in a certain manner, the theme stubbornly insists upon developing itself in its own way, and any attempt by the poet to wrest it from the peculiar or even erratic course proves either abortive or disastrous to the poem as an inspired work of art.

"One has often had the experience, while revising a word or phrase, that the right word or phrase is throbbing upon the borderland of consciousness. You know and feel that such a word or phrase is about to be presented to you by the Unseen Hand, and at last is magically flicked into your brain, as the inevitable, yet all-needful, trifle that makes Perfection."

George Bernard Shaw asserted that *St. Joan* was written by Joan herself. Here are his own words: "As I wrote, Joan of Arc guided my hand, and the words came tumbling out at such a speed that my pen rushed across the paper and I could barely write fast enough to put them down."

Though he stated that he was a hardened old professional who was inspired all the time during his working hours, Shaw added: "My subjects

come to me anyhow, and when I have chosen
my subject, the play writes itself. I can even
begin without a subject with the same result.
The characters come and talk and define themselves and explain their business, and there is
your play for you. Thus my plays must be
classed as inspirations, not as constructions."

In his preface to *Buoyant Billions*, written
when he was ninety-two, he says: "When I take
my pen or sit down to my typewriter, I am as
much a medium as Browning's Mr. Sludge or
Douglas Home, or as Job or John of Patmos.
When I write a play I do not foresee nor intend a
page of it from one end to the other; the play
writes itself."

Cosmo Hamilton tells a remarkable story con-
cerning the last scene of his play *Scandal*. He
spent hours "niggling with words," but all of
them were wrong. The scene was proving too big
for him. Finally, he admitted defeat and prayed
for inspiration. This was the sequel:

"Very soon I found myself cooler and probably
saner than I had been and perfectly happy,
writing easily and without any correction, until,
after ten pages or so had been covered with
dialogue, the word 'Curtain' wound them up.
Then I went to bed, and when, with the most
intense eagerness I read, early the following

morning, what I had written, I knew that there was not a single word that came out of my brain. My pen had been used. I had been heard and helped, and what had been written for me during that hour was so far above anything I had ever written as to be unrecognisable to me."

Dr. Alexis Carrell sums up inspiration thus: "Great discoveries are not the product of intelligence alone. Men of genius, in addition to their powers of observation and comprehension, possess other qualities, such as intuition and creative imagination. Through intuition they learn things ignored by other men, they perceive relations between seemingly isolated phenomena, they unconsciously feel the presence of the unknown treasure.

"All great men are endowed with intuition. They know, without analysis, without reasoning, what is important for them to know. A true leader of men does not need psychological tests, or reference cards, when choosing his subordinates. A good judge, without going into the details of legal arguments, is capable of rendering a just sentence. A great scientist instinctively takes the path leading to a discovery. This phenomenon, in former times, was called inspiration."

The fact that many distinguished authors

received their plots in dreams demonstrates that the mind, even if it be only its subconscious part, continues to function despite the body being asleep. J. W. Dunne has earned fame for his book, *An Experiment With Time*, in which he proves that the mind acquires knowledge during our sleep state that it not available when we are awake. His attention was first aroused by a series of vivid dreams in which he foresaw the future.

Dunne began to experiment, keeping a note-pad by the side of his bed, recording, as soon as he awoke, the events he had dreamed. He found that unless he made his record immediately on awakening, while the events were still in his memory, the dream recollections speedily vanished. Soon he was able to record a number of prophetic dreams which were fulfilled. This was conclusive evidence that during sleep the mind lived in another dimension of time, because it was able to experience the future. His book demonstrates this other time-dimension by a series of remarkable mathematical diagrams.

Dunne evolved, as a result, what he called his theory of Serialism, which stressed that man was more than a body. His mind was more powerful than his physical senses, obviously superior because it was not subject to the restrictions im-

posed on the normal sense perceptions. From
that, he concluded logically there was no reason
to assume that the superior mind should perish
with the death of the inferior body, and some
form of mental survival beyond death must be a
fact.

Dunne's book provides an explanation of the
means by which inspiration is sometimes accomplished. In sleep, when the senses are stilled and
the noise of the busy world is hushed, the mind
is able to attune itself to the more delicate and
subtle vibrations which permeate the universe.
Responsive minds can be impinged by higher
beings who seek this opportunity of enriching our
world with their added knowledge and wisdom.
And it may well be that the mind is receptive,
during bodily sleep, to other incarnate minds
operating on a similar wavelength.

Sleep, of course, is an essential part in the
divine plan, providing the body with needed rest
and the opportunity of recuperation. While the
physical world is stilled, the mental and spiritual
worlds are active. Indeed, they can only become
active when conditions are appropriate for their
functioning. When the physical world is noisy
with its many clashes, discords and clangours, it
is virtually impossible for our mental and
spiritual natures to find expression.

I know, as you must do, people who have been perplexed by difficulties to which they could not find the solution. They have thought about them all day, and then in the morning the perfect answer has been awaiting them when they awoke. The inner and outer forces have been at work and provided the answer. Confronted with alternate choices of action, the solution can often be found in "sleeping on the problem."

It must be appreciated that inspiration and guidance from higher sources come through the subconscious and not the conscious minds. We have not yet discovered all the tremendous potentialities of our subconscious natures. Just as the subconscious mind will perpetuate bad habits, so, given the necessary stimulus, it will equally acquire good habits. Mental discipline is necessary to encourage the latent creative faculties to get to work. The mental training adds exhilaration to life and supplies the preparation needed to obtain help from the unseen.

The fact that one man receives inspiration means there is a law which makes it possible to happen. Laws do not operate for one man alone. They will operate for all who provide the necessary conditions. You, too, can be inspired when you are receptive, when your mind is attuned to the higher forces.

CHAPTER X

THE GLORY OF LIFE

THERE are times in life when everything you do turns out well. You radiate health and energy. Life is full of sunshine; there are no clouds to darken your horizon. There are other periods when everything goes wrong. You appear to be living in a world of darkness, with bad fortune and illness dogging your footsteps.

The explanation in each case is simple. You are either in harmony with the natural laws, and so are at one with the universe, or you are not. The results follow automatically.

Instead of being an aimless cork tossed on the ocean of life, you can fulfil your part in the great plan by understanding the purpose of your existence. Development of character is an essential part of the divine scheme.

The majority of people pay far too much attention to the body. It is paradoxical but true that the best way to develop self is to forget yourself. This is another way of saying, "He that loseth himself findeth himself." If a fraction of the care lavished on the body were devoted to the development of the mind and spirit, life would become a greater and richer adventure for the majority of mankind.

The body has certain primary needs which must be satisfied. It requires clothing, food, air, exercise, rest and shelter. Once these fundamental needs have been supplied, superfluous material possessions are merely chains that impede the individual's real progress. Most people eat far too much and certainly more than is required to sustain their bodies. The purpose of food is to replace lost energy and to build the body.

During the last war, when severe rationing was imposed, there was not, as some feared, an increase of disease. On the contrary, better health was enjoyed by the vast majority. The virtues of fasting have been proved by people we describe as saints throughout the ages. It is one method by which individuals become more accessible to higher influences, because they are in control of their bodily appetites and can rise above them. Who has not heard of nature-cure establishments where health is restored by fasting for days and even for weeks?

More people die from over-eating than from starvation or malnutrition. In all factories, care is taken to give vital machinery some rest to prevent it from wearing out. Yet the human body, with its wondrous mechanism, is expected to continue its work, day after day, the whole year round, without respite. Too often it breaks down under the strain.

Gandhi, that great Indian and mystic, realised how few were his primary needs. His clothing was reduced to a minimum, as were his food and drink. His possessions were almost nil. The fact that he was frequently imprisoned did not affect him, for he could continue the same mental and spiritual life in jail as he could outside it. Because he was already mentally and spiritually free from earthly chains, prison could not diminish his real liberty. It could not rob him of anything he required to sustain him. Because he had nothing he had everything.

The truth is that the more you know about the higher forces the less you find you want. It is the ignorant individual who thinks he is important because his possessions are many. His sense of values is false, his perspective is out of focus.

First things must come first. If your mind and spirit are in tune with the universe, everything else will fall into its allotted place. You will not want.

The bounty of God is lavish and often prodigal.

There is an abundance of all that we require to sustain us. The essentials of life are either free or the cheapest that can be bought.

It is normal and natural to enjoy good health, which will follow automatically if your thinking is right. When your thinking is right, your living will be right. Illness, sickness and disease are abnormal. They are caused by man living out of harmony with nature. They are the price to be paid for what we regard as civilisation.

Man has almost divorced himself from the natural forces which bring health and vitality. The result is to be seen, for example, in the astonishing fact that every year more and more people are compelled to wear spectacles in early youth and to be deprived of their teeth.

Our food is highly chemicalised and robbed of its natural vitamins. Have you ever considered how your life is influenced, to a great degree, by the commercial advertising of certain foods? To take one example, the public has been made to believe that white bread is superior to brown. Flour has been sifted more and more thoroughly and so deprived of its most useful components. This treatment allows it to be preserved for longer periods and facilitates the making of bread. Millers and bakers earn more money.

The consumers eat an inferior product, believing it to be a superior one. According to Dr. Carrell, in countries where white bread is the principal food, the population degenerates. Enormous sums are spent on publicity, with the result, he says, that "large quantities of alimentary and pharmaceutical products, at the least useless, and often harmful, soon become a necessity for civilised man."

Let me quote another authority, Dr. Magnus Pyke, who was a Principal Scientific Officer at the Food Ministry, author of the Government's official *Manual of Nutrition* and accepted as a leading expert on general nutrition in this country. In his book, *Townsman's Food*, he states that nearly ninety per cent. of British flour is still being treated with a bleaching agent which makes it poisonous to dogs, rabbits and possibly to human beings. This is slowly being put right, but the practice, started in wartime, of adding fourteen ounces of chalk to every sack of National flour still goes on.

In France, not long ago, I asked a woman why I seldom saw brown bread on sale in her country. She replied that there was so little demand for it, except in the very large towns. Then she hesitated and inquired, "What do they do to the flour to make it brown?" Though she was an

4*

intelligent woman, she had not realised that brown was the natural colour of wheat.

In ever-increasing quantities, chemicals are poured into the earth in attempts to achieve quicker results. The less natural food we eat, the more the body is deprived of its resistance to illness and disease. There is no adequate substitute for natural foods.

In this twentieth century of civilisation, millions of people regularly swallow drugs which they think will cure them or prevent illness. Drugs do not and cannot cure. They are suppressive in action. In any case, they deal with effects and symptoms, and not with causes. Some drugs are merely stimulants that provide an unnatural acceleration of certain bodily functions, but a price has to be paid. Too often, unfortunately, the price is that the heart will not stand the strain of this constant acceleration.

Smoking, drinking alcohol and taking narcotics are not natural activities. They produce deleterious effects in the bloodstream and, though the doses may be small, people who indulge in these habits immoderately are literally absorbing poisons whose cumulative effect is injurious.

It is worth quoting Dr. Alexis Carrell, who

THE GLORY OF LIFE 103

says that medicine is far from having decreased human sufferings as much as it endeavours to make people believe. The years of life which have been gained by the suppression of diseases like diphtheria, smallpox and typhoid fever are paid for by the long sufferings and the lingering deaths caused by chronic affections, and especially by cancer, diabetes and heart disease.

"Although modern hygiene has made human existence far safer, larger and more pleasant," he writes, "diseases have not been mastered. They have simply changed in nature."

He points out that there are two kinds of health, natural and artificial. Scientific medicine had given man artificial health and protection against most infectious diseases. This was a marvellous gift. But man was not content with health that was only lack of malady and depended on special diets, chemical products and the constant attention of surgeons, doctors and nurses. Man wanted natural health, which came from resistance to infections and degenerative diseases, from equilibrium of the nervous system. He wanted to live without thinking about his health.

Few people give the body its natural healthy exercise. The motor car is both a boon and a curse. While it provides an easy and quick means of transport, it encourages laziness and prevents people from walking. When God fashioned the body, He gave us legs so that they should be used. When limbs are not exercised, in time they lose their usefulness. The more muscles work, the more they develop. Activity strengthens them, instead of wearing them out. Organs atrophy when they are not used.

Speed is a very mixed blessing. Only posterity will be able to judge whether the aeroplane is to be regarded as a help or a hindrance to mankind. In any case, too many people are in a hurry to get nowhere. They boast of the time they save, and having saved it they do not know what to do with it. Only a tiny minority know how to relax, so that their limbs obtain complete rest. Their muscles, like their minds, are nearly always in a state of tension.

Machinery enables man to work fewer hours, but the increasing leisure is not utilised in pursuits that enhance the mind or spirit. Craftsmanship, with its love of making beautiful objects, is almost a thing of the past.

Fear of illness, which is so rampant, encourages illness. Newspapers are full of advertisements persuading people to buy drugs and pills that are supposed to prevent or to palliate diseases of varying kinds. These advertisements, unfortunately, encourage the fear-complex. A healthy mind has nothing to fear and a healthy body will repel all adverse factors. Besides, once the drug-taking habit has been formed, it is hard to break it.

Once I had in my employ a man with an extraordinary fixed idea that he was always sitting in a draught. The slightest breath of air in the room was sufficient to make him panic. Day after day, he complained of a stiff neck caused by sitting in a draught, though other people in the same room felt no ill-effects. His fear made him a bundle of nerves and he became a sick man whom nobody could cure. Fresh air is good for us. The trouble is that we do not get enough of it, and that the only air we habitually breathe is far from fresh. Besides, a healthy body cannot be affected by draughts.

It is important to realise that clean thoughts are as essential as clean bodies. Right thinking is the first stage in right living. Mental training and discipline are evidence of self-control and prove that we are not merely drifters. We think, whether it be consciously or unconsciously, before we speak or act. Thoughts of anger, hatred and revenge are bad for the thinkers of them, apart from those against whom they are directed. They betray the mental and

spiritual poverty of the individuals responsible
for them and poison their minds and bodies.

Bernard Shaw's secretary tells of an occasion
when she received a letter full of venom about
her employer. When she showed it to G.B.S., he
merely smiled and shrugged his shoulders. She
said that Shaw could not feel malice towards
anybody because he was at peace with himself.
In a life filled with controversy, he never gave
vent to spite or rancour.

Like attracts like. That is true in the mental
and spiritual aspects as it is in the physical one.
Hatred, anger and revenge poison the mind,
impair its efficiency and rob it of the power to be
attuned to higher forces. They pollute the
atmosphere just as effectively as fog.

Those gifted with inner sight can see the aura
that surrounds every individual. It follows the
contour of the body and is composed of a series
of emanations. It is a complete index to the
owner's character, health, attainment and progress, as depicted by differing colours. Thoughts
of malice and revenge have a marked effect by
isolating the individual from all the greater
forces around him. The "lines of communication"
contract and the "web" closes in.

From the lowest standpoint, self-interest
dictates the folly of meeting hatred with hatred.

Higher considerations show that by doing good to those who hate you a great victory is won over self and a decisive step forward is taken on the road to attainment. Only those who are abysmally ignorant of the higher laws are able to indulge in hatred. Those who have the knowledge realise that hatred is a boomerang. Great souls cannot hate.

Hate begets hate, just as love begets love. It is easy to desire revenge. To demand an eye for an eye and a tooth for a tooth is to respond to the lowest instincts. It is also the equivalent of the individual constituting himself prosecuting counsel, judge and jury, and it rules out any suggestion that he himself might be wholly or partially in the wrong. Usually, in any dispute, there is something to be said for both sides. Neither is completely right nor completely wrong. Experience proves that issues can seldom be resolved into black or white, and that in most cases they are grey.

Kipling understood the implications of hatred when he wrote that if you could be lied about and "don't deal in lies, or being hated, don't give way to hating," then "yours is the earth and everything that's in it."

The founder of Christianity gave what he described as a new commandment, "Love one another." That is difficult enough, but he went further and set a higher standard, loving our enemies. It is not easy for an evolving mankind to reach this ideal, but as it strives towards its attainment it is improving itself, and the rest of the world.

Nurse Cavell realised this great truth after a life of sacrifice and devotion. When she was about to face the firing party, she gave voice to the profound declaration, the first half of which is only quoted: "Patriotism is not enough. I must have no hatred in my heart for anybody."

When that ideal is achieved, the individual has won his greatest victory. He has peace within and without. He draws everybody towards him, fearing none and desiring only to help others. He has made himself accessible to the highest he can reach. He has become attuned to the greatest souls in the universe, because he has established kinship with them. Self has been conquered because he desires nothing, for having love he has everything. "Love," it is said, "is the fulfilling of the law."

It is easy to love your own kith and kin when you feel a natural affection for them. That is no hardship. It is easy to love those to whom you are attracted by ties of mutual interests and sympathy. It is not easy to love those who do not love you and for whom there is no warm or tender feeling. But that represents the greatest advance in character and in the development of mind and spirit.

In Leigh Hunt's poem, when Abou Ben Adhem asked the angel what he was writing in his book of gold, he was told, "The names of those who love the Lord." Ben Adhem said, "I pray thee, then, write me as one that loves his fellow-men." Later, the angel showed him that in his chronicle "Ben Adhem's name led all the rest."

As the higher aspects of your nature unfold, you find that life is full of unexpected joys. Among them is the great joy of giving, rather than receiving, without expecting gratitude; giving because you have reached the stage when you desire to enrich the lot of others.

Character is strengthened when you can stand on your own feet, realising that your strength comes from within and without. I have never forgotten this verse which a friend quoted to me:

> "The glory of life is to love,
> Not to be loved;
> To give, not to get;
> To serve, not to be served;
> To be a strong hand to another in the
>   time of need,

> *To be a cup of strength to a soul in a*
> *crisis of weakness,*
> *That is to know the glory of life."*

Do not waste time or energy in regretting lost opportunities, or in self-pity because of any personal sorrow. You cannot alter the past or the present. You can mould the future.

Carmel Myers, a former Hollywood film star, has written an inspiring book, *Don't Think About It*, which describes how she conquered her own sorrow and obtained a new perspective on life. She had made a success in films and enjoyed great happiness from her marriage which lasted for twenty-two years. It ended suddenly one evening when her husband died.

"I was utterly unprepared for the dreadful suddenness of the blow," she writes. "When the immediate impact of horror had passed, I found myself caught in a whirl of self-pity that grew worse with every passing day."

The sympathy and consolation expressed by friends did not help her. They were constant reminders of the pain she was experiencing. She could not obtain comfort from religion.

Feeling that she must find a remedy of her own that would remove her despair, she decided to close the door on the past. With her three children, she moved from Hollywood to New York to face the challenge of the future alone. Her reason told her: "There's nothing I can do to change what has happened. Thinking about what I would like undone in the past will not help me in any way. So I must stop thinking about it."

In a spirit of mingled jest and sorrow, she started, for herself alone, a Don't Think Club, with the motto, "If you can't help it, don't think about it." Determined not to be left on her own, which provided too many opportunities for contemplating the past, she sought new friends to whom she outlined her philosophy.

Instead of meeting with scoffing or patronage, she found, to her surprise, that they were responsive and accepted her point of view. "It is a matter of closing off your mind like a switch," she said, "like hypnotising yourself to forget. It means crowding every minute of your day with some activity."

After a few months, when the passage of time, as it mercifully does, was slowly healing her own ache, Carmel Myers had seven friends who were sharing the motto of her Don't Think Club. Each had a private grief, but when they met they studiously ignored it. The moment one of them detected a break in the voice, or a drift into self-pity, they would call the weaker member to order, insisting that the club's rules be observed. Gradually, everyone felt a new confidence. They were all able to pick up the threads of life again, regarding each day as a new adventure. The Don't Think Clubs grew in small groups as other people caught on to the idea.

When it was suggested to Carmel Myers that her philosophy was a form of escapism, that she was encouraging people to flee from reality, she sought the opinion of a competent psychologist. He observed that her slogan would be bad advice in cases where there was a hidden layer of guilt, when people felt that in some way they were responsible for their tragedy. Otherwise, he failed to see how any self-respecting psychologist could object to her philosophy. He added that a few friends, who shared the sorrow of personal suffering, could build a common wall of protection against the lowness of spirit that comes from grief.

Misery is not permitted in the Don't Think Club. Members are not allowed to wallow in their own or anybody else's sorrow. The whole purpose is to rise above grief, not to linger with it.

Many people derive a morbid pleasure from their sorrow. They enjoy the self-imposed martyrdom which gives them a kind of import-

ance that they never previously felt. Their grief
takes possession of them. After all, it is not so
much what happens to you that matters, but
how you deal with it.

It took Carmel Myers two years to fight her
way out of the darkness and emptiness to a
living fullness. "The first step is the hardest to
take," she says, "but it is a short cut to peace of
mind. When you stop being sorry for yourself,
you are on the road to helping yourself." Her
new outlook led her to realise, "It is hardship
rather than comfort, failure rather than success
that warms us to our fellow-creatures."

Her philosophy is another way of saying that
you get out of life just what you put into it; no
more and no less. Anything else would be
contrary to divine justice.

Motive is always a consideration. It is plati-
tudinous but nevertheless a fact that you cannot
do better than your best. If, having done so,
subsequent events do not favour you, then at
least your motive was right and you have been
consistent with the highest ideal of conduct. You
cannot be blamed for the consequences. If, however, your motive was selfish, and things turn
out badly, you have only yourself to blame for
the result.

During the last war, when, month after month,

Britain and her Allies faced a dreary procession of disasters, Winston Churchill records that he consoled himself with the reflection that he had, so far as he knew, done his best, mortals could do no more and one day the tide would turn. Strangely enough, soon after he gave vent to these reflections, he received news of the first change in our fortunes. From that time, there followed a catalogue of triumphs.

When you have self-confidence, and you are living in accordance with the highest that you know, you can face whatever each day will bring. You know that every experience helps to develop your character and makes you better able to appreciate the glory of life.

CHAPTER XI

"More things are wrought by prayer than this
world dreams of"

PRAYER can play an important part in your life. You must, however, appreciate all that is involved in prayer. The poet James Montgomery answered the question, "What is prayer?" by writing:

> *"Prayer is the soul's sincere desire,*
> *Uttered or unexpressed,*
> *The motion of a hidden fire*
> *That trembles in the breast."*

Can prayer achieve results that could not have been obtained by any other method? Are prayers heard and answered?

When a Harley Street specialist announces that he has obtained, solely by means of prayer, cures which could not have been achieved through orthodox medical means, this is the kind of testimony that must be considered. It is impossible to dismiss prayer as wishful thinking in the face of such a pronouncement.

The specialist, Dr. Christopher Woodard, was so impressed with these cures, achieved by some higher power, that he announced his intention of relinquishing most of his London practice and of devoting five days a week to faith healing. Dr. Woodard, who is known to many Olympic athletes, has a remarkable story to tell. Part of it was given when, by permission of the padre, he addressed a group of students, doctors and nurses in the chapel of a London hospital.

He described the dramatic cure of his own son, who, at the age of two, was stricken by one of the worst cases of fulminating meningitis he had ever seen. The physician in charge gave the child only a few hours to live, and said that if he survived the mind would become unbalanced. Dr. Woodard told how he took his son's hand and prayed. He believed that this case, so close to his own heart, involved a test of his faith. "My faith was upheld," he said. "My son was cured." The boy subsequently went to school, and its reports cited his extremely high intelligence, thus disproving the physician's prognosis.

Another case Dr. Woodard quoted concerned a woman suffering from cancer. One night, while a guest at a priest's house, the woman went to bed feeling extremely ill. The priest laid his hand on her and prayed earnestly. Soon, the woman was fast asleep. At three o'clock the next morning, she declares that she was awakened by a blaze of light in the form of a cross. The malignant growth had gone and she felt and looked twenty years younger.

This same priest was asked to help a man whose leg was to be amputated. Purely as a result of the power of prayer, declared this specialist, the dreaded operation was averted. The man, however, was left with a condition of sciatica, which he reported to Dr. Woodard when next he visited his consulting room. The medical man, following the priest's example, resorted to prayer, with the result that the patient was cured.

Dr. Woodard, interviewed by a newspaper, told of an occasion during the war when he served in minesweepers. He came across a blind sailor and prayed for the man to be helped in his affliction. Months later, he learned that the sailor regained the sight of one eye almost instantly.

In his address at the chapel, he urged medical people to adopt a positive frame of mind when they treated the sick. If they allowed themselves to think that cases were incurable, they were obstructing the healing rays. He asserted that where doctors and nurses had faith, there was no limit to what could be done.

This specialist's attitude to prayer doubtless owes some of its origin to the fact that he is the son of an Anglican priest. He has realised that God provides sufferers with a second chance when skilful medical men pronounce the dreaded verdict, "incurable." He declared that it was not a snap decision, but a long belief in the power of prayer which led him to become resident medical director and to devote most of his time to treating patients at Milton Abbey, Dorset, the Anglican sanctuary of healing, where priests and doctors co-operate.

The Rev. Leslie Weatherhead, the well-known Methodist minister of London's City Temple, has, for many years had the help of doctors at his clinic where healing by prayer is effected.

I have already made a brief reference to the cures at Lourdes, which I visited some years ago. I thought the Grotto itself was impressive, though some of the surroundings, particularly the shops, were meretricious. Dr. Carrell has written that certain spiritual activities might cause both anatomical and functional modifications of bodily tissue and organs.

He says of the cures recorded by the Medical

Bureau of Lourdes that our present conception
of the influence of prayer on "pathological lesions
is based upon the observation of patients who
have been cured almost instantaneously of
various affections, such as peritoneal tuberculosis, cold abscesses, osteitis, suppurating
wounds, lupus, cancer, etc. Sometimes, functional disorders vanish before the anatomical
lesions are repaired." He adds that the only
condition indispensable to the occurrence of this
phenomenon is prayer. But there was no need
for the patient himself to pray, or even to have
religious faith. It was sufficient that someone
around him was in a state of prayer.

How far can prayer help human life? What
are the laws behind its operation? Why do some
prayers succeed and others fail? These questions
are not easy to answer because we know so little
about the mechanics of prayer. It is foolish to
suggest that every form of medicine or healing
should be discounted and patients encouraged to
rely solely on prayer or faith to achieve cures.
Every type of healing has its own contribution to
make in the cure and alleviation of sickness. The
important point is that results *are* achieved by
prayer when all known methods have failed.

The fact that prayers are answered means that
some intelligence is responsible for the resulting

cures. Something or somebody hears the prayers and puts into operation certain forces which transcend medical treatment.

Prayer must not be regarded as a substitute for action. It is a prelude and a preparation for action. It is a means of obtaining results in times of crisis or emergency. Sufficient has already been written in these pages to show that man has access to higher powers and that the material world is only an infinitesimal part of the universe.

Prayer sometimes has a potency for which there is ample evidence in the lives of thousands of people. The results obtained seem to depend on the nature of the prayer and the person who prays.

Dr. Muller, who was in charge of a Bristol orphanage, declared that he never begged for contributions. He prayed for the money required to maintain his orphanage and he asserted that it was always forthcoming.

The Rev. John Maillard, the well-known faith-healer, declares that answers to prayer provided him with the money needed to buy Milton Abbey, with its one hundred rooms and eight hundred acres, near Blandford, Dorset, where he has his Sanctuary of Healing.

In 1936, he began to search for a suitable house. Milton Abbey was suggested. It had

recently passed from a banking family to the
Ecclesiastical Commissioners. The price asked
was twenty thousand pounds.

After discussing this house with the Bishop of
Chichester, who had appointed him to take
charge of the first Church of England mission of
healing, he wrote a circular letter to the seven
thousand members of the Fellowship of Inter-
cessors who had been linked up in prayer with his
healing mission. In this letter he asked for
prayers that the money should be received.
"Within six months," he says, "I was standing
in the Abbey with a cheque for twenty thousand
pounds in my hand."

Two years later, he declares, the same source
provided a further fourteen thousand pounds for
the building of an extra wing to the Abbey.
"Now," added Mr. Maillard, "we live financially
from day to day." The Abbey costs fifty-five
pounds a day to maintain when it is full and
thirty-three pounds when it is empty.

Some years ago, I received some extraordinary
evidence which clearly proved that a sincere
prayer, uttered by a broken-hearted woman in
Blackburn, was brought to the notice of a group
of people in a London suburb, two hundred miles
away. Yet they had no knowledge of the woman's
existence, let alone her prayer. I made a detailed

investigation of the circumstances and was satisfied that it was a case of answer to prayer.

Sincerity is the keynote to prayer. God is not impressed because words of more than one syllable are used or because the petition is couched in a copy of biblical language. Neither is it necessary to remind the Infinite Intelligence of your needs or the things that you think should be done. Obviously, Infinite Intelligence, as these words imply, knows about them even before you have spoken.

In some cases, the best service is rendered to the petitioner when he does not get the response he wants at the time, because, although he may not know it then, his request will not add to his mental and spiritual growth. Selfish prayer always defeats its own ends.

Nevertheless, true prayer cannot be a waste of time. It opens the door by which the answer can come. When you have exhausted all your efforts to find a solution to your problem, then you have a right to seek aid from higher sources. This type of prayer, and the one which desires that the petitioner should unfold his latent talents to be of some service in the world, become a spiritual exercise which attunes the individual to the higher forces. It compels introspection; the individual examines his weaknesses and honestly desires to learn how he can become a better citizen, in every sense of the word.

I do not suggest that prayers are heard by a personal God, for I do not accept such a conception, and certainly not in the sense in which personality is usually understood. Though it states in Genesis that God made man in the divine image, it is true that ever since man has returned the compliment.

I believe that in the answering of prayer Jacob's ladder, with its numerous intermediaries, is utilised. Some of these beings have constituted themselves our guardian angels, a theme to which I shall return in subsequent pages. In real prayer, we draw close to them, because we are allowing our mental and spiritual faculties to express themselves, and these provide the bridge by which we reach them. Sincerity gives wings to prayer and aids it on its flight through the invisible worlds. There can be no cheating, or pretence, for all is known and a true assessment made by those who are competent to do so. They read us like an open book.

There are some who declare, as a result of long study of the forces employed, that verbal prayer is preferable to the silent variety. They aver that when petitions are made orally, the speaker is compelled to concentrate. This immediately

checks the wandering of thoughts and the intro-
duction of other ideas which so often happen to
Westerners who lack the ability to meditate.
The number of individuals who can maintain
their thoughts on one specific theme for any
length of time is very small. It has also been
suggested that sound itself creates a helpful
vibration. To appreciate any aspect of mental
and spiritual life, you must recognise that you
are dealing with realms in which vibrations play
an important part.

Though I frequently use the phrase "mental
and spiritual realms," I wish to emphasise that
these are not worlds that are completely separated from their physical counterpart. The
universe is one in which every aspect of life
blends. At any given moment, we manifest in
varying worlds, material, mental and spiritual,
though we are still in the same universe. There
is no real separation between matter, mind and
spirit.

What many people call the spiritual world is
not situated in some distant part of the universe.
It has no specific geographical location. You are
as much in the spiritual world today as ever you
will be. You are no nearer to it in an aeroplane
and no more distant in a submarine.

Not only do all aspects of universal activity

blend, they are also constantly reacting on one another. You cannot make separate compartments of matter, mind and spirit. What affects you materially will also affect you mentally and spiritually. And it is equally true that what affects you spiritually will affect you mentally and materially.

The laws which control matter, mind and spirit also blend with one another. There cannot be any contradiction between them because they are regulated by Infinite Intelligence.

All these laws continue to operate irrespective of your views, religion, or beliefs. They are impartial and mechanical in their behaviour. A cork tossed on the ocean must float and a stone must sink. So far as we can tell, these natural laws have always been in operation. And so far as we can hazard a guess, they always will be in operation.

They operate with mathematical exactitude. There are no miracles in the sense that there is interference with their operation. This would be a reflection on the infinite wisdom, which is responsible for them, for interference suggests eventualities that were not foreseen.

The laws do not reward or punish, in the sense of bestowing favours or sending tribulations. If you are in harmony with them, you automatically reap the result, which could be described as your reward. If you are out of harmony with them, you automatically reap the result, which, perhaps, in one sense, is your punishment.

You cannot influence the operation of natural laws. They are subject to cause and effect, which must achieve their inevitable sequel. Effect is compelled to follow cause, in itself due to a previous effect. And so, link by link, the endless chain is forged as part of an inexorable process.

Nothing can be more striking than the contrast between man-made laws and the natural ordinances. Human beings can cheat man-made laws because these cannot control every circumstance in life. They cannot cheat natural laws. What is sown must be reaped, and that is true of every aspect of natural law. There can be no mistakes.

Some years ago, when I had a cottage in the country, I took pride in our garden, experiencing the joy that comes from the closer touch with nature when you grow your own vegetables, fruit and flowers. I remember planting seeds from a packet which was labelled "ridge cucumbers." To my surprise, the result was marrows! But the natural laws had not made a mistake. The packet was wrongly labelled and contained marrow seeds, which had no alternative but to grow according to their nature; effect had to follow cause.

While we cannot, because of our human limitations, comprehend infinity, we can obtain a glimpse of the divine intelligence behind life when we contrast the laws of man with those of God. Frequently, Parliament has to revise, modify and abandon ancient statutes because, in their original forms, they no longer apply to changed conditions. New circumstances constantly arise that demand the making of new laws.

When these are debated, no matter how cleverly they were framed, or how wise the minds of those who drafted them, skilful lawyers are able to point to defects and to suggest remedies, which other astute lawyers oppose because of faults that they enumerate. The result is frequently a compromise. And by the time a Bill has become an Act of Parliament, it is often found that modifications are necessary.

Yet the natural laws, which regulate every activity in a boundless universe, continue to work with perfection. The tides ebb and flow, the planets pursue their allotted courses and the earth rotates on its axis. These stupendous phenomena occur with a mathematical precision that awakens wonder and reverence in the minds of beholders. The movements of the tides can be ascertained for years ahead. The position of every planet can be equally determined. Provision has been made for everything in the universe. All is regulated by natural laws which never err, falter or forget. They continue their task ceaselessly.

Compared with the minds that evolved man-made laws, how infinite must be the intelligence responsible for all the laws of nature! It is foolish to think of this overriding power in terms of a person, and to limit it to the male sex. It is equally foolish to imagine that God possesses nationality, or is a member of any particular religion. Just as God must be infinite, so there must be an infinite number of approaches to the divine fountainhead.

None can possess a monopoly of divine wisdom, or compel it to flow through any special channel. No book, however sacred, can contain the whole of infinite inspiration. No church can be large enough to capture the whole of infinite intelligence.

Edgar Wallace, who rightly achieved fame because of his thrillers, once had a remarkable dream. He found himself in heaven in the company of a number of venerable, bearded sages who were examining the most beautiful diamond he had ever seen. In some mysterious fashion he knew it was the diamond of Truth. It was flawless and shone with crystalline brilliance.

Then a tragedy occurred. While being handled by one of the sages, the diamond slipped and fell to earth, where it shattered into a thousand fragments. Where each splinter fell, a group of people excitedly acclaimed it and used it as the foundation on which to build a church. Each group maintained that it possessed the whole of divine truth. The sages gazed at this spectacle with dismay tinged by humour, for they knew that not until all the fragments were reassembled could the whole of divine truth be made known.

The fact that you open your mind to receive more truth means that you make yourself more accessible to those who are capable of supplying your needs. The Bible statement, "He shall give his angels charge over thee, to keep thee in all thy ways," is based on a truth. From the moment of your birth there are attached to you, through bonds of affection or kinship, beings who have volunteered to guide you. These are your guardian angels, though I must stress that they are human beings and not winged figures. Sometimes they are related to you by ties of blood or family. Sometimes they are kindred souls, attracted because they see in you a means of giving service to your fellows.

These guardians cannot absolve you from the responsibilities of your actions. Their function is to guide, not to rob you of your initiative or free will. They are competent to guide because of their extended vision. They are familiar with the path you are treading because they once trod it themselves. And they have experience of the higher spheres towards which you are inevitably making your way.

They strive to influence you to derive the best from life, and not to make the mistakes that they may have done. Their guidance is also directed towards ensuring that you should not chase after illusions but find reality.

Sometimes, when you are in tune with them, you become aware of their conscious guidance; too often, unfortunately, it is unconscious and you are unable to feel their presence. The fact that you do not see or hear them is no argument against their nearness. There is much in the universe that you cannot see or hear. A blind man cannot see a sunset, but it exists. A deaf man cannot hear the song of birds, but they do sing.

Often the reason for the services rendered by

these guardians is due to their love for you. Love, which is stronger than death, is the most powerful force in the universe. I am, of course, referring to real love, and not to the distorted versions often found in novels, on the stage and depicted in the cinema. Passion and infatuation are not love. True love expresses itself on all planes of being, physical, mental and spiritual.

Contrary to the Anglican marriage service, those whom love has joined cannot be separated. Death does not part them. A husband and wife, who do not love one another, are mentally and spiritually parted, even though they still share the same house and the same name.

Those who love you in the Beyond regard it as a privilege to help you, just as you would gladly aid those you love. This explains one of the means by which prayer is answered.

Many people assert that should they find survival after death to be true, they will be glad to be freed from any association with earth, with all its cares, troubles and headaches. If, however, they have left behind someone they love, this will provide the strongest incentive to keep close to them and to help them through the rest of their earthly journey, until the glory of reunion is their mutual lot. Whatever vistas of beauty the hereafter may offer, it is no sacrifice for a loved one to delay his exploration and stay with his beloved.

All this is so aptly summarised by Shakespeare's "There's a divinity that shapes our ends, rough-hew them how we will." Evolution has proved that man is part of an ascending order of being. This, coupled with a realisation of the wondrous provision made by the natural laws for every form of life, including our own, reveals the beneficent purpose that broods over all. The vast cosmic scheme is a revelation of divine wisdom and love.

You can share its ineffable qualities as you make yourself more responsive to the overruling will and power expressed in all creation. You can participate in its eternal processes. Your responsibility and free will, however restricted they may be, decide whether your lot is a heaven or a hell, both here and hereafter.

The natural law of cause and effect determines that the saint and the sinner, to give an example, cannot have an equal spiritual status. The gulf is fixed by their own behaviour and character. Were it otherwise, divine justice would be a mockery.

The purpose of life is to build a character that is fitted by a variety of experience for the next inevitable stage. Earth is a school where you learn your lessons and receive your training for the greater existence beyond. None can live your life for you. No other shoulders can bear your responsibilities. It is no use worrying about what other people do, or say, or think. That is not your responsibility. You are responsible for what you do, say or think. Whatever good you do, you are the better for it. Whatever sins you commit, you are the worse for it. That is cause and effect in operation.

There is an old Spanish proverb, "Take what you want, says God; take it, and pay for it." You cannot have something for nothing. You must be prepared to pay the price. Life will provide both compensation and retribution. You can always rise higher because there must be room for betterment in a life of eternal progress. Do not boast or be smug, because as high as you have risen so low can you sink. And if you are living in the valley of the shadows, you can comfort yourself with the reflection that things could always be worse. Besides, it gives you the opportunity of a wonderful achievement by rising to the top.

There is no situation in life that is completely bright or abjectly dark. When you have scaled one peak, another peak, hitherto unseen, becomes visible to your new surroundings. The more you

5*

attain, the more you realise there is to be attained.

Guided by knowledge, the wise individual will seek the eternal riches in the spiritual truths that, once obtained, can never be lost. No one can rob you of spiritual truths. That is where they essentially differ from material possessions. The acquisition of knowledge is one of the most important pursuits in life.

Where knowledge is obtainable, it is always preferable to faith, which, too often, is blind and credulous. You are better equipped when you have knowledge rather than ignorance. Ignorance is the jailer who imprisons your mind. Knowledge is the key which sets your free.

Knowledge cannot take you all the way because there are realms in which faith is essential. Not all the higher truths can be revealed in our present state of evolution. But then the new faith will be founded on a greater knowledge.

CHAPTER XII

THE KINGDOM OF HEAVEN

YOUR philosophy must take account of death, for it is inevitable. The refusal to recognise that death must come, or repeatedly to defer consideration of it, is foolish and short-sighted. So important an event cannot be ignored.

Some people refuse to make a will because they believe that by so doing they will hasten their demise. A well-known American doctor writes, "How often we find that the victim of a 'sudden' and unheralded heart attack has been consulting his lawyer about his will, or has recently taken out a new life-insurance policy."

There are few certainties in life, but death is one of them. You cannot refuse to die, just as you could not refuse to be born. And you do not know when you will be called upon to pass the bend in the road into the country beyond. The wise individual recognises these inescapable facts and moulds his life and philosophy accordingly.

I saw in a newspaper, the other day, a letter in which the writer said: "Without doubt the death of a loved one is the most shattering experience that can befall the human spirit. There is no theory or formula which can deaden the immediate overwhelming pain of bereavement.''

Those who possess a knowledge of spiritual truths realise that all mourning is selfish. We are bemoaning our own physical loss. No tears should be shed for those who have escaped from darkness into the light, freed from all the diseases, infirmities, inequalities and injustices of earthly life. For them, it is an occasion for rejoicing at their promotion from the kindergarten to the larger schoolhouse. No one should want to stay in the kindergarten for ever.

Armed with knowledge, you do not fear the coming of death. You recognise that it is an essential step in the order of life, just as much an integral part of existence as birth. One provides the entrance into the physical world and the other the exit.

Those who have given no thought to the higher and deeper aspects of their being, and have devoted the whole of their lives to materialistic pursuits, will, as a result, be unprepared when death comes. They will be like travellers who are ignorant of a country they are bound to visit. The individual who realises that he is merely passing from one form of existence to a larger one faces daily life with serenity and confidence because he knows his future destination.

I know a man who, when he is asked, "How are you?" startles his questioners by replying, "I am a day nearer death than I was yesterday." I have a friend, a lecturer on spiritual matters, who surprised one audience by telling its members that they were all potential corpses. It was not the most tactful of comparisons, neither was it calculated to gain him sympathy, but the statement was true, at least, so far as their bodies were concerned.

Many people have obtained glimpses of this future existence and always they have described it in terms of wonder and beauty. They found there was nothing to dread. These experiences occurred in times of serious illness, when the inner faculties opened. Their owners became aware of the larger life and even saw some of its denizens, whom they recognised as loved relatives or friends. Such an experience befell the wife of Bernard Shaw when she lay dying. It made a profound effect on her husband, for it was contrary to the views on the life-force he had expounded for years.

Sir Patrick Hastings, the eminent counsel, had a similar glimpse of the hereafter. He found it so attractive that he almost regretted his return to this life and declared it made him realise that death had no terrors.

Sir Oliver Lodge, the renowned scientist, who devoted over fifty years of his life to investigating the operation of the invisible laws that control the spiritual forces, found that his new knowledge deepened his reverence for the supreme intelligence directing the universe. His scientific researches made him more religious, though not in a specific orthodox sense.

He was once called as a witness in a lawsuit and was cross-examined on his views on spiritual matters. When it was suggested to him that what previous witnesses had described as the spiritual world was an illusion, he shook his head. "This is the world of illusion," he answered; "reality is to be found only in the invisible."

This striking declaration confirms that true science cannot contradict true religion. Indeed, one of the great tragedies of the world has been the conflict between science and religion. In the past, when religion persisted in its belief in miracles and in tenets that stretched faith almost to its limits, it met the opposition of scientists who refused to accept any doctrines which could not be proved by materialistic methods. Thus, the philosophy of materialism spread, with the worship of science as its new god.

Early scientists refused to recognise an unseen world or invisible forces. They asserted that matter, which was indivisible, was the only reality. Modern physics, however, concerns itself largely with forces so minute that not even the most sensitive apparatus can detect their existence. Nuclear fission has forced on us the uncomfortable truth that a tremendous power exists in the invisible.

Science, which previously would not concern itself with the application of its discoveries, has now brought mankind to the cross-roads of destiny. The atomic bomb poses a question mark which concerns the whole of humanity's future, for good or ill. The dilemma arose because, under the impetus of war, science discovered a weapon for which humanity was not spiritually ready. Thus science had forced on itself the necessity for recognising spiritual implications. And the gulf between science and religion has been narrowed.

The twentieth century, however, is faced with a dilemma which has been ably summarised by General Omar Bradley, who writes: "With the monstrous weapons man already has, humanity is in danger of being trapped in this world by its moral adolescents. Our knowledge of science has clearly outstripped our capacity to control it.

We have too many men of science; too few men of God. We have grasped the mystery of the atom and rejected the Sermon on the Mount.

"Man is stumbling blindly through a spiritual darkness while toying with the precarious secrets of life and death. The world has achieved brilliance without wisdom, power without conscience. Ours is a world of nuclear giants and ethical infants. We know more about war than we know about peace, more about killing than we know about living. This is our twentieth century's claim to distinction and to progress."

By one of the strangest paradoxes, man, through the advance of science, and not religion, has been compelled to think in terms of spiritual necessities. Recognition of the higher and deeper forces is being forced upon the consciousness of man. We are now compelled to consider the truths enshrined by all the founders of religion.

The doctrine of materialism, which is responsible for selfishness and ultimately leads to war, is now exposed in all the nakedness of its folly. Even hard-headed and so-called practical individuals are being forced to realise that selfishness does not pay either individually, nationally or internationally. Altruism is the best policy, even from the viewpoint of self-interest!

The solution of the many problems which confront us demand an understanding of the fundamentals of our existence, the realisation that we are mental and spiritual beings and that we cannot escape from this reality. General Bradley has emphasised in modern language what was enunciated two thousand years ago, "Except ye become as little children, ye shall not enter into the kingdom of heaven."

We are beginning to discover that the spiritual maxims propounded by religious leaders are very practical and cannot be ignored if man is to fulfil the true purpose of his being. To "become as little children" does not envisage a return to childhood. It bespeaks the necessity for simplicity. Man complicates his existence by his alleged civilisation.

I cannot improve on the simple but sublime declaration, "Seek ye first the kingdom of God, and His righteousness; and all these things shall be added unto you." This is a bold statement, but it is true. Once you realise that the kingdom of God, which is the kingdom of heaven, can be found, and you live your life in harmony with that knowledge, all "these things" that you need are automatically added. You face each day with tranquillity, equanimity, serenity, calmness and confidence. You are certain that as long as you are faithful to the knowledge you possess, you cannot be let down.

Knowledge brings responsibility, which challenges you as to the use you make of knowledge. Your offence is greater if you are selfish, greedy or avaricious when you have knowledge of the working of natural laws. That, I believe, is the real interpretation of the many biblical references to the "sin against the Holy Ghost." The word "ghost" in its original really means spirit. You are offending against the spirit when your behaviour is contrary to your knowledge of spiritual realities.

Throughout the world, there are many thousands who live in the daily awareness of the guidance to be obtained from the forces that are both within and without.

I remember one man who told me, some years ago, that he had opened "a joint banking account" with God. In times of difficulty, he explained, God allowed him to overdraw the account, but he always had to replace it because it was a joint account. He maintained that all his needs were constantly supplied.

The natural laws always achieve harmonious results. Visit any beautiful garden where there is a profusion of flowers and, though there may be hundreds of different hues, they aways blend, a tribute to the Infinite Intelligence whose supreme artistry can never be duplicated by man. Similarly, the whole of universal activity moves with rhythm and concert, each aspect fulfilling its allotted task.

The key to health, happiness and a rich full life is to be found only by living in harmony with the universe and by realising that you are an essential factor in the great scheme. Do not regard yourself as insignificant or of no consequence. Your existence is evidence that you have a contribution to make.

Never forget that you are essential to the divine scheme. The fact of birth provides you with all the equipment that you require, physically, mentally and spiritually. Just as minute invisible cells, with which your body originated, contained part of your physical organism, even to the shape of your fingernails, so at the same time you were endowed with your mental and spiritual equipment. It is your own fault if you do not use all the armoury that God has supplied. It is there as part of your divine heritage.

Your entry into this world also provides you with an unbreakable link with God, and you require no intermediary. No event in life or death can sever that bond. Within you are the

means by which you can have access to the
infinite storehouse.

You are as much a part of God as God is a part
of you. You contribute, by your existence, to
the nature of divinity. In miniature, you possess
all that the Infinite Spirit has. You are one of the
threads in the divine fabric.

CHAPTER XIII

"WHERE IT LISTETH"

YOU cannot command help from the higher forces. All you can do is to put yourself in the right condition to receive it. There is a saying in the East that when the pupil is ready the master appears. When you are spiritually ready, the higher powers will reach you.

"The wind bloweth where it listeth." It is obeying the laws responsible for its operation. It cannot and does not make mistakes. The power of the spirit, which the higher forces utilise, is reaching out always to find responsive channels through which to flow.

Being spirit, the dynamic of life, the essence of creation, it takes many forms. It is the divine fire which consumes the artist as, almost in a frenzy, he follows the unmistakable commands that come to him from the unseen. He has not called down the power. By a set of circumstances over which he has no control, the time and place are right and he is receptive.

One clergyman sits in his study, consults books of reference, makes copious notes and finally writes his sermon. Though it may be full of scholarship, classical allusions and display his knowledge of foreign languages, it does not move his hearers.

Another clergyman makes no preparation. He goes into the pulpit without any notes and speaks "as the spirit gives him utterance." He captures his congregation from the start. They recognise that he is inspired, the mouthpiece of some higher force that is responsible for the eloquence that provides food for their souls.

Every speaker and writer knows when he has been inspired. He recognises the tremendous difference between his laboured, stilted performances and those in which he has been the vehicle for the subtle forces which enable the right words to flow effortlessly from him. I remember that once, while seated in a cinema, watching a gangster film, the opening words for a leading article came into my mind. Hastily, I took a scrap of paper and wrote them down, knowing from past experience that, unless inspiration is recorded immediately, it vanishes and becomes almost impossible to recapture. That evening, before I went to sleep, I took a note pad, placed it on my knees, wrote down the words I had heard in the cinema, and immediately the rest of the leading article was written. The result was not in my normal style. The words had a beauty of expression and rhythm which, alas, I have found it difficult to duplicate.

Words are the most elusive tools. There are only twenty-six letters in the alphabet. Shakespeare wrote sonnets with them, while the majority stumble and fumble to find the right words to express shades of meaning. But then the Bard's pen was kindled by the divine flame to a degree that has never been equalled. The beauty of Shakespeare's prose and verse is that every word is in its rightful place and it is impossible to substitute another for it—a profound tribute to the inspiration of which he was the instrument.

A friend of mine, a gifted speaker and a writer, who was conscious of the source of the inspiration which came to him, was able to practise telepathy regularly with his wife, a phenomenon which he proved to me on one occasion. He told me that he could always distinguish between telepathic impressions and those which came to him from higher sources. He illustrated the difference by saying that the telepathic communications were like being prodded with a stick, while the inspired messages were more akin to a warm breath on his brow.

This always made me think that inspiration is

related to the creative forces of life. After all, the literal meaning of "inspire" is to "breathe in," which, of course, is life, while to "expire" is to "breathe out," which is death. When you are inspired, you are "breathing in" the more subtle forces of life.

Unfortunately, man has always sought to canalise and to restrict the higher forces, to compel them to flow into channels of his making. The history of religion is one long conflict between inspiration and theology, or, put another way, between the ideas of God and those of men.

The founders of every world religion were individuals who were inspired from on high. They were moved by the power of the spirit. Their followers sought to limit the divine revelations, to codify them, to make them conform with accepted beliefs, to reduce them to orthodox tenets. Theology supplanted inspiration. And so it became necessary for another burst of inspiration to descend, to reinstate what had been smothered by the orthodox whose one concern was to try to force the new wine into old bottles.

There are too many living today who are afraid to stray beyond the accepted idea. They are wedded to Orthodoxy. Their minds and souls are closed. They feel safe behind the walls they have erected. The familiar, however barren and sterile, is enough for them. New ideas are not welcomed. They are afraid of them. They resist the new just because it is new. They cling to the old just because it is old. They are scared of being disturbed. Adventure is not for them.

What was good enough for their father is good enough for them, they will tell you. Or they boast, "I have always held these opinions and I will always hold them." What they really mean is that these opinions will always hold them. But nature abhors a vacuum. You must either go forward or backward. Rigidity is death. The closed mind is a curse in every aspect of life. The story of progress is one long fight between new ideas and old fears in art, religion, literature, economics, medicine and, indeed, in every form of human activity.

Knowledge, like truth, is infinite. Nobody knows everything. Knowledge has to be pursued and attained. It will not come to you without effort. The son of a scholar inherits no knowledge from his father. He has to seek it for himself. The son of a philosopher does not inherit philosophy from his father. He must acquire it for himself. The mind does not unfold spontaneously. It must be used and stimulated. The more it is exercised, the more proficient it becomes. The less it is exercised, the less efficient it will be.

Knowledge does not conform to material laws. When you share it with another, you have not lost anything. On the contrary, the process of sharing will enrich you, for you learn more in so doing.

Reason is a divine gift. God gave you the ability to think and you are intended to use your reason. To accept tenets or doctrines, because others have believed them for years, when they seem unreasonable to you, is to betray your divine inheritance. A rigid mind is as harmful as a hard artery. They both spell death.

Learn to open out, to unfold all your faculties, spiritual, mental and physical, to the maximum of their development. That is how you qualify for the "more things in heaven and earth." The sunflower turns its face to the sun, the source of all its strength, growth and life. Turn to the infinite power, the source of all your strength, growth and life.

You cannot live without the power which fashioned you, which made you in its divine image and which has made provision for all your needs. Live with it. Harmonise your will to the divine will. Allow its radiance to flood your being.

Once you have united yourself with the divine plan, life becomes rich, full and abundant, simply because you have harnessed yourself to the infinite source. You receive the divine illumination which transcends all physical sense. Your life is then guided, from hour to hour, by the greatest power in the universe. You have come into your own. You have learned to have perfect confidence in the laws behind life, knowing that they cannot fail.

You, too, will then say, "The Lord is my shepherd; I shall not want." All your inner faculties, stimulated by the power within and without, will be at work. Your inner eyes will see. Your inner ears will hear. You will not fear or flinch because of problems or difficulties. You will *know* that as they arise, guidance will provide an immediate response and solution. You will *know* what is best for you to do.

You will learn how to retire into the silence of your own soul and to listen to the voice of divine truth, always striving to make itself heard by those who have ears to hear. You will be able to distinguish between illusion and reality and not mistake the husk for the kernel. You will know what it is to feel radiantly alive, to welcome every new day with zest because it provides opportunities for fulfilling your part in the divine plan.

You will not cringe, demean yourself, boast or be vainglorious. True humility will be yours. You will walk in the light and not in the shadows, conscious always of the everlasting arms around you, knowing that you are wrapped in the cloak of divine love.

As you become more receptive to higher forces, so your body become less coarse. Refinement of mind and soul lead to refinement of body. Grosser foods will not appeal. Your appetite will change and your body will demand more delicate sustenance. You will not require the artificial stimulants that so many think are essential to their welfare.

You will have discarded much useless lumber, material, mental and spiritual, that has cluttered up your life for too long. You will know the difference between your wants and your needs. You will have rid yourself of much that is superfluous, a thousand and one encumbrances that civilisation had foolishly persuaded you were essential to your being. You will not retain what you cannot use. You will know that you were not intended to be a glutton, a miser or a hoarder.

Life will be brighter, happier, richer, fuller and healthier because you know how to live. Having found the way, you will desire to share your joys with others, so that they may learn how the infinite power, to which you attune yourself, is always present and always in operation, just like the natural laws, which never fail to regulate all universal activity.

This infinite power is waiting to illuminate them and everybody else in the world. It is always available, without charge, anywhere and at any time, making no distinction between colour, caste, creed, clime, language, race or nation. It is God's greatest gift to humanity, the means by which it can establish the kingdom of heaven on earth.

PL 457936

SHOP JM2080   A/N/PS AQUA PB   BIN 1311H

WHERE THERE IS A WILL   £3.50   ISBN 0850307538

05/07/88   BARBANELL,M

Other recommended reading

LIVE LIFE FIRST CLASS

Kenneth Thurston Hurst

Down-to-earth, easy-to-understand methods you can apply *immediately* to solve day-to-day problems and get the most out of life.

- 5 guidelines to increase your prosperity consciousness
- How to apply the law of attraction
- Improve your health and develop 'wellness'
- Learn how to really enjoy life

The natural order of life is change. You *too* can change. You *can* become the successful and confident person you want to be. **Kenneth Thurston Hurst** explains all.

HOW TO BE HEALTHY, WEALTHY AND WISE

M H Tester

We live in times of stress and uncertainty, where materialism is the god of the majority. We need to recapture the lost art of living, to experience freedom from sickness and frustration. But how? Prayer is not enough — what we need is a DIY manual. This is it! Written in simple, easy-to-read style, this book shows how to get and keep healthy. It also demonstrates how to become successful and wealthy, and gives practical advice applicable to every problem every day.

TIBETAN SECRETS OF YOUTH AND VITALITY

How to Look and Feel Younger Using Five Rites for Stimulating Your Energy Centres

Peter Kelder

For hundreds of years the monks in Tibet have daily practised specific exercises — or rites — said to improve health, restore youth and increase life-span. Although remarkably simple to perform, because they act directly upon the seven chakras or energy centres of the body, their effects are remarkable. **Peter Kelder's book is the first ever English presentation of these rites.** *Fully illustrated.*

THE KI

Takashi Yoshikawa

An easy-to-read but precise instruction manual on how YOU can use the ancient energy of the Ki to ★ **solve problems** ★ **fulfil your ambitions** ★ **achieve true peace of mind.** Hundreds of years ago the Chinese discovered a correlation between the energies of earth, water, fire, metal, wood, and time cycles with the basic numbers 1-9. Here Takashi Yoshikawa presents a simple table for you to look up your individual number, then shows how to read off your personal destiny predictions based upon yearly and monthly cycles. *Illustrated with charts and diagrams.*

WHAT IS ENLIGHTENMENT?

John White

Most of us probably think of it as some sort of spiritual state or experience, and that's fine as far as it goes — but what does enlightenment *feel* like? Does it mean understanding ALL things, or is it simply a deep and profound insight into one aspect of life? — and while we're on that problem, IS there more than one aspect to life? To KNOW would be to experience enlightenment, but we CAN approach that experience through the writings and teachings of men popularly regarded as enlightened. **John White** presents the personal insights of: Aldous Huxley; J. Krishnamurti; Evelyn Underhill; Sri Aurobindo and others. *Endlessly thought-provoking and challenging.*

UNITIVE THINKING

Tom McArthur

Unitive thinking is a system of 'side-stepping' a problem to gain a different perspective and increase possible options. The technique itself is not new, what IS new is the growing awareness of this radically different approach to life. **Tom McArthur's** easy and comfortable approach explains the basic concepts and shows how they can be used to:

- Overcome limitations, biases and prejudices
- Achieve greater all-round awareness
- Improve practical skills

It also clearly illustrates the very real link between modern, mystic and scholarly schools of thought. *A demanding yet 'fun' book particularly relevant to the problems of today's world.*